MW00782893

Baking for Two

Baking for Two

The Small-Batch Baking Cookbook for Sweet and Savory Treats

Tracy Yabiku

ROCKRIDGE
PRESS

Copyright © 2016 by Tracy Yabiku

No part of this publication may be reproduced, stored in a retrieval system, or transmitted in any form or by any means, electronic, mechanical, photocopying, recording, scanning, or otherwise, except as permitted under Section 107 or 108 of the 1976 United States Copyright Act, without the prior written permission of the publisher. Requests to the publisher for permission should be addressed to the Permissions Department, Rockridge Press, 918 Parker St., Suite A-12, Berkeley, CA 94710.

Limit of Liability/Disclaimer of Warranty: The publisher and the author make no representations or warranties with respect to the accuracy or completeness of the contents of this work and specifically disclaim all warranties, including without limitation warranties of fitness for a particular purpose. No warranty may be created or extended by sales or promotional materials. The advice and strategies contained herein may not be suitable for every situation. This work is sold with the understanding that the publisher is not engaged in rendering medical, legal, or other professional advice or services. If professional assistance is required, the services of a competent professional person should be sought. Neither the publisher nor the author shall be liable for damages arising herefrom. The fact that an individual, organization, or website is referred to in this work as a citation and/or potential source of further information does not mean that the author or the publisher endorses the information the individual, organization, or website may provide or recommendations they/it may make. Further, readers should be aware that Internet websites listed in this work may have changed or disappeared between when this work was written and when it is read.

For general information on our other products and services or to obtain technical support, please contact our Customer Care Department within the United States at (866) 744-2665, or outside the United States at (510) 253-0500.

Rockridge Press publishes its books in a variety of electronic and print formats. Some content that appears in print may not be available in electronic books, and vice versa.

TRADEMARKS: Rockridge Press and the Rockridge Press logo are trademarks or registered trademarks of Callisto Media Inc. and/or its affiliates, in the United States and other countries, and may not be used without written permission. All other trademarks are the property of their respective owners. Rockridge Press is not associated with any product or vendor mentioned in this book.

Photography © 2016 Stockfood/Great Stock!, back cover (right) and p.2; Stockfood/Gräfe & Unzer Verlag/Julia Hoersch, p.6; Stockfood/Alain Caste, p.9; Stockfood/Philip Webb, p.10; Stockfood/Alexandra Grablewski, p.22; Stockfood/Martina Schindler, p.56; Stockfood/Micah Beree, p.86; Stockfood/Mark Thomas, p.112; Stockfood/Jean-Christophe Riou, p.134; Melina Hammer, cover and p.156; Stockfood/ Tanya Zouev, p.196; Stockfood/George Blomfield, back cover (left) and p.220.

ISBN: Print 978-1-62315-792-0 | eBook 978-1-62315-793-7

To my mother and all the other teachers, in the classroom and out, who have touched my life. You shape the world. Thank you.

Contents

Introduction

Growing up, baking from scratch wasn't a huge part of my daily life. I learned the basics, with Mom's hands over mine, making batches of cookies from a recipe on the back of the chocolate chips bag. And I have fond memories of my grandmother's kitchen, stirring oil and eggs into boxed cake mixes. Baking was a fun weekend activity.

Moving into my first college apartment, I brought with me a solid chocolate chip cookie recipe, the belief that the only frosting worth using contained tiny rainbow chips and came in a can, and the certainty that baking anything more complicated than a drop cookie required magical powers I did not possess.

But college has a way of eroding certainties and, to combat my homesickness, I turned to baking in my little galley kitchen. I learned that, sure, there is some magic to baking a toe-curlingly good cupcake (but that power is mostly science) also patience and care, and not mixing up the baking soda and baking powder. It was something I could do, something I loved. So I did it a lot.

My twenties is a story written in frosting and sugar, with sticks of cinnamon and quarts of good vanilla. I devoured new recipes (and their results), learned everything from everyone I could, and tried new baking techniques. During those years, there was always a new batch of delicious somethings cooling on my counter.

Alas, I gained 20 pounds. People around me put on weight. It became obvious: The way I was running my kitchen, churning out huge batches of baked goods, was unsustainable. So, to adopt a healthier lifestyle, I began downsizing my kitchen output.

Creating small-batch recipes was fun and challenging, and I still ate new and delicious foods—but in a responsible fashion. Now everyone is healthier, and my friends and family appreciate more the special things I occasionally bake for them.

In 2015, I created my blog, *Baking Mischief*, as a place where I could share my recipes and cooking adventures. The following pages contain some of my favorite small-batch recipes, along with tips, tricks, and simple step-by-step instructions. Every recipe here—from humble shortbread cookies to a decadent chocolate soufflé—was created with the everyday home cook in mind. I can't wait for you to try them.

CHAPTER ONE

Good Things Come in Small Packages

Whether you're watching your carb and calorie intake, trying to eliminate food waste, or just really sick of having leftovers, small-batch baking is the perfect, easy, and delicious solution to your kitchen woes.

Before we get to the small-batch recipes, let's consider why they're a good idea and take a quick look at some of the tools, ingredients, and techniques we will use to create them.

Downsizing

The size of the average household in America is shrinking. We are staying single longer and having children later. More and more we find we don't need—or want—recipes that serve a crowd. Giant casseroles and cookies by the dozens suit a family of six, but in small households, they often go to waste or sit there tempting you to overindulge.

Cutting down those recipes is fine, in theory, but if you've ever tried to quarter a cookie recipe you know it is not always easy. More often than not, particularly with baking recipes, they don't divide evenly. You have to split an egg, figure out how to quarter one-third cup of butter, and adjust cooking times because, whatever you are cooking, there is less of it. A small miscalculation can ruin a tried-and-true favorite.

With the recipes here, I eliminate the guesswork for you. All are properly scaled, timed, and tested for smaller baking yields, so your baked goods come out perfectly each time.

Scaled-Down Equipment

Small-batch baking doesn't require a lot of specialized equipment, just some scaled-down cookware. Invest in good-quality pieces and they will last a lifetime. Baking requirements vary somewhat from recipe to recipe, but the following equipment is used for the recipes in this book.

Small Skillets and Saucepans (Mini skillet and 1-, 2-, and 3-quart saucepans) Mini (6-inch) cast iron or other ovenproof skillets are used for baking some dishes right in the skillet, such as the perfect Skillet Peach Cobbler (page 118); small- and medium-size skillets are used for cooking some ingredients on the stove top, especially for savory dishes, before being combined with the remaining ingredients.

One-, two-, and three-quart saucepans are ideal for small-batch cooking. The 1-quart size is perfect for making caramel and other dessert sauces, and the 2- and 3-quart sizes are large enough for boiling pasta.

Loaf Pans (3-by-5½-inch mini and 9-by-5-inch medium) The standard size for mini loaf pans is 3 by 5½ inches, and they're often sold in sets of two to four. While glass and ceramic pans look pretty and are better for certain types of baking, you will have the best results using metal pans for the quick breads in this book. A medium-size loaf pan (9-by-5-inch) is great when you can freeze the extras, like brownies and blondies.

Pie Pans (6 inch) A 6-inch pie pan makes a perfect savory quiche, or dessert pie for two to three people. Glass versus metal is largely a matter of personal preference—they both have their pros and cons—and either will work fine for the recipes we will be making.

Cake Pans (6-inch round) Six-inch round pans make a cake that serves two to four people. Look for pans at least 2 inches deep with straight sides. This gives you the option of making a single cake tall enough to cut into layers.

Tart Pans (4¾ inch) Mini tart pans make perfectly adorable single-serving tarts. Save yourself a lot of pain and cursing, and buy pans with removable bottoms to make sure your tarts can be removed perfectly and intact every time.

Ramekins (5, 8, and 12 ounces) It's nice to have a few sets of ramekins ranging in size from 5 ounces to 12 ounces. The smallest size is perfect for crème brûlée and individual soufflés, and the larger ones can be used for everything from single-serving casseroles to individual potpies. For the recipes in this book, you will need 5-ounce, 8-ounce, and 12-ounce ramekins.

 **Baking Dishes (3-cup, 5-by-7-inch rectangular)** A 3-cup, 5-by-7-inch baking dish will make a generous two-serving casserole, cobbler, or small sheet cake. You can buy some lovely stoneware and ceramic dishes, but Pyrex is a great budget option. It's inexpensive, versatile, and excellent for storing leftovers.

 Springform Pan (4½ inch) A springform pan is a cake pan with a removable bottom and sides that clamp into place. It is used for delicate and custardy dishes, such as cheesecakes, that can't be inverted to be removed from their baking containers. We will be using 4½-inch pans for the cheesecakes in this book.

 Bundt Pan (1-cup mini) Mini Bundt pans produce single-serving cakes in a variety of fancy shapes. They are ideal for pound cakes, and vary in size from ¾ cup to 1 cup.

 Muffin Tins (standard and mini) We will use both standard and mini muffin tins for the recipes here. Heavy-duty non-stick tins give you a nice, even cooking experience and make for easy cleanup. Purchase one with handles, or plenty of space on the sides, for easy handling.

Baker's Pantry

If you keep a well-stocked baking pantry, you always have the basic ingredients on hand to whip up something delicious. Specialty ingredients come and go, but these staples are the foundation of most baking recipes.

Baking Powder and Baking Soda Baking powder and baking soda are both leavening agents—they help baked goods rise. They serve nearly identical functions in baking recipes, but don't try to substitute one for the other in a one-to-one ratio (baking soda is about four times more powerful than baking powder, but requires an acid to activate it). Both should be stored in their original containers in a cool, dry place and, as a rule of thumb, replaced every six to twelve months.

Kitchen Essentials

The following are the essential tools every home baker needs, whether baking for a household of one or a family of six.

- BAKING SHEETS
- COOLING RACK
- DRY MEASURING CUPS
- KITCHEN SCALE
- LIQUID MEASURING CUP
- MEASURING SPOONS, INCLUDING ⅛ TEASPOON
- MIXING BOWLS
- PARCHMENT PAPER
- ROLLING PIN
- RUBBER SPATULA
- SIFTER
- WHISK

Specialty items, which fall into the nice-to-have category, include silicone baking mats, pastry blender, pastry brush, handheld electric mixer, food processor, biscuit cutters, a kitchen torch, and candy and oven thermometers.

Butter Butter is used in the recipes here and its incomparable qualities and flavor make it the star ingredient for baked goods. Butter can be kept safely at room temperature for short periods of time, but should be refrigerated for long-term storage. Shortening can often be used as a substitute, but flavor and texture might suffer. Never automatically substitute one for the other. When in doubt, follow the recipe as written.

Chocolate The most common types of baking chocolate are unsweetened, bittersweet, and semisweet. Bittersweet and semisweet can be used interchangeably. Recipes often specify a cocoa percentage, which refers to the amount of chocolate that comes directly from the cocoa bean. Generally, the higher the percentage, the darker and less sweet the chocolate. Improperly stored chocolate can become dull and splotchy. To ensure that your chocolate stays fresh and delicious, store it in a cool, dry place, out of direct sunlight, and away from strong odors, which chocolate can absorb. Don't store chocolate in the refrigerator because it develops "bloom," a dull gray film from the cocoa butter separating from the chocolate. The flavor is not affected.

Cream To some degree, whipping cream and heavy (whipping) cream can be used interchangeably. The difference is in the amount of fat. Whipping cream contains at least 30 percent milk fat, and heavy cream at least 36 percent. The higher fat content means heavy cream will produce a slightly more stable finished product when whipped, but both work fine as toppings on desserts and in hot beverages. Cream should be refrigerated and used within two weeks of opening.

Eggs The FDA recommends that eggs be kept refrigerated and used within three weeks of purchase. Unpasteurized eggs should not be consumed raw or undercooked because of the risk of foodborne bacteria; pasteurized eggs may be safely used in dishes and toppings when the eggs are not cooked.

Flour The most common types of flour used in baking are all-purpose (bleached and unbleached), whole-wheat, bread, and cake. Generally, flour substitutions can be made, but the different types of flour are not interchangeable and substitutions almost always result in a change of texture for the finished product. White flours should be stored in a cool, dry place, preferably in an airtight container to keep out bugs. Whole-grain flours should be stored in an airtight container in the freezer to prevent their natural oils from going rancid.

Read the ingredients lists closely when they call for sifted flour. One cup of sifted flour is not the same as 1 cup of flour, sifted. Sifting fluffs up the flour, so 1 cup of sifted flour will weigh less than 1 cup of flour, sifted. This may seem like a small point, but baking is organic chemistry, and it can be the difference between success and failure.

Sugar The sugar used in this book is granulated, superfine (also known as caster), powdered (or confectioner's), coarse (or sanding), and brown. Granulated sugar is the common white granules you think of when you think "sugar." Superfine sugar is granulated sugar further processed to create granules that dissolve quickly. Powdered sugar is sugar that has been ground to produce a fine powder. Coarse (sanding) sugar is a large-crystal sugar mainly used for sprinkling on top of baked goods to give it a lovely, sparkly appearance. Brown sugar comes in light and dark varieties, and is granulated sugar with molasses added; the light and dark labels refer to the amount of molasses added. Some recipes call for one type or the other, as dark brown sugar has a slightly stronger molasses flavor, but they can mostly be used interchangeably. Sugar should be stored in a cool, dry place away from strong odors.

Vanilla Extract and Vanilla Beans Vanilla extract is made by infusing a mixture of alcohol and water with macerated vanilla beans to produce the dark amber liquid that makes cookies taste so good. Vanilla beans can be on the pricey side and are ideal in recipes when you really want the vanilla flavor to shine through.

Both types of vanilla should be stored at room temperature (never in the refrigerator) in a dry place out of direct sunlight.

Baker's Dozen

A baker's dozen is thirteen—everyone likes a little extra treat! So, here are my top thirteen rules to help you be the happiest, most successful baker you can be.

1. READ THE INSTRUCTIONS FIRST—ALL THE WAY THROUGH. It's tempting to dive right into a recipe and start baking, but reading the instructions all the way through before you begin can be the difference between success and disaster.

2. PRACTICE MISE EN PLACE. *Mise en place* is a French culinary term meaning "everything in its place." Before you start cooking, prepare your workstation. Get your equipment ready. Measure ingredients and have everything cut and ready to go. This enables you to make the recipe without interruption and you will never get halfway through preparing a cake only to realize you are out of eggs.

3. MEASURE PROPERLY, PREFERABLY WITH A SCALE. We will discuss this more in Baking School (see page 18), but proper measuring techniques can be the difference between a perfect cupcake and a cupcake tragedy.

4. SUBSTITUTE WITH CARE. Substitutions and modifications are encouraged. They can really make a recipe your own, but baking, unlike cooking, is highly dependent on chemical reactions, and requires careful research before you do any substituting of flours, sugars, and fats. Altering a recipe without understanding the chemistry involved is the fastest way to disaster.

5. SHARE. Share the things you make. Share your recipes. Share the baking experience. Life will be richer (and tastier) for it.

6. CLEAN AS YOU GO. Cleaning is never fun, but it's even less fun when a dirty kitchen is standing between you and your chance to enjoy a plate of freshly baked cookies. Clean as you go, and your kitchen will be ready when your cookies are.

7. BUY THE GOOD VANILLA. It makes a difference, and you're worth it.

8. REMEMBER IT DOESN'T HAVE TO BE BEAUTIFUL TO TASTE GOOD. Sometimes lattice crusts go awry and cookies decide to merge into one big cookie in the oven. They might not look perfect, but they'll still taste perfectly delicious.

9. GIVE YOURSELF MORE TIME THAN YOU THINK YOU NEED. Sure, that recipe says it takes one hour, and most of the time it will. But the one time it doesn't will be the one time company is knocking at the door while you're still fighting with your pie dough.

10. DON'T MAKE A RECIPE THE FIRST TIME IN A HIGH-STAKES SITUATION. For giant roasts and elaborate cakes, this is easier said than done, but small-batch recipes like the ones in this book are very doable. Save yourself some stress by testing recipes before special events, so you can bake with confidence when it matters.

11. TRUST YOUR INSTINCTS. Yours are good. Listen to them when they say those cookies are ready to come out of the oven two minutes early.

12. IF YOU'RE WRONG . . . LEARN FROM YOUR MISTAKES. Enjoy those slightly doughy cookies (they taste better that way), remember that baking "disasters" (or mishaps) are part of the joy of cooking, and, next time, take those cookies out one minute early.

13. LICK THE BOWL. Do it responsibly. Don't give yourself food poisoning, but life is short.

Baking School

Baking is fun and often simple, but it can also be unforgiving. Proper technique is important and can make the difference between a light and airy cake and one that's more hockey puck than dessert. These are the techniques you will need to know to bake everything in this book.

Achieving Room Temperature (Butter, Cream Cheese, and Eggs) The easiest way to bring butter, cream cheese, and eggs to room temperature is to allow them to warm on the counter for 30 minutes to 1 hour. If you are short on time, submerging eggs in warm water for 5 to 10 minutes will bring them to room temperature. For butter, cut sticks into ¼- to ½-inch cubes and allow them to sit at room temperature while you prepare and measure the rest of your ingredients. You know the butter is the right consistency if you can easily leave an indentation with your finger but the rest of the butter still holds its shape. Cream cheese can be cut into small strips or cubes and left on the counter to help it reach room temperature more quickly. It may separate if you try to heat it in the microwave or with another heat source, so plan accordingly.

Avoid Overmixing Overmixing can result in tough, chewy baked goods. Pay close attention to the instructions. When the recipe says, mix "just until combined," it means just combined. Stir ingredients together just until you no longer see distinct streaks in your batter. Lumps are expected and fine!

How to Grease a Pan You have a couple of options when it comes to greasing pans. Cooking spray is quick and convenient, but it can leave behind residue that will build up on your pans over time, leaving them discolored. I usually reserve cooking spray for aluminum foil-lined baking sheets and my ancient, battered muffin tins. To avoid damaging your nicer bakeware, use butter or shortening for greasing. Soften a stick of butter on the counter or use room-temperature shortening, and a pastry brush, paper towel, or sheet of wax paper to spread a very thin layer of butter or shortening over the sides and bottom of your pan.

How to Butter and Flour a Pan To flour a pan, first grease the pan with butter (or shortening) as described above, and add a couple tablespoons of flour (or cocoa powder if you are baking a dark cake). Gently shake the pan until the entire bottom is coated. Then rotate the pan so the flour falls to the side, and turn the pan a full 360 degrees so the entire interior of the pan is coated.

I like to add parchment paper to the bottom of my cake pans so I can be absolutely sure my cakes come out clean. Simply trace around the pan on a piece of parchment paper and cut on the inside of the line to ensure the parchment paper will fit inside your pan. Butter the parchment paper and press it (butter-side up) securely onto the bottom of the floured pan before adding the batter.

Cutting in Butter Cutting in butter is essentially breaking butter down into smaller pieces and incorporating them into your dry ingredients. A pastry blender, which can be purchased for less than $10, will give you the quickest, easiest results; you can also use a fork, two knives, or your fingers. To use your fingers, simply rub very cold butter and flour between your fingers, continuously breaking down the butter chunks until they reach the size called for in the recipe, usually pea size.

Folding Folding is usually called for when you want to combine two ingredients without losing the volume of one of them, for example, when adding whipped egg whites to cake batter. To fold, use a large spoon or plastic spatula and literally fold the batter over on itself. Run the spatula around the bottom and pull the batter up and over the other ingredients. Rotate the bowl a quarter way at a time with your free hand and repeat. Do this carefully and only as much as needed to combine the ingredients without deflating the mixture.

Measuring Liquids Liquids can be measured accurately in either wet or dry measuring cups. Place measuring cups on a level surface and fill either to the brim for a dry measuring cup, or to the correct measuring line for a liquid measuring cup. Because dry measuring cups must be filled to the brim to be accurate, a liquid measuring cup is preferable, and potentially less of a messy option.

Measuring Dry Ingredients The most accurate way to measure dry ingredients, especially flour, is by weight with a kitchen scale because 120 grams (4.23 ounces) of flour always weighs 120 grams, but 1 cup of flour is not always 1 cup of flour since flour can be compressed depending on how you handle it. A scale allows you to be accurate and will also make your baking go much quicker because you won't have to stop and search for the correct measuring cup sizes for every ingredient.

The weight of different baking ingredients varies quite a bit. For example, 1 cup of powdered sugar weighs 120 grams, while 1 cup of granulated sugar weighs in at 200 grams. Once you start baking by weight, the weights quickly become second nature; in the meantime, you can refer to the chart on page 222 for the equivalent weights of common baking ingredients.

If you do not own a kitchen scale, the next best option is to use a large spoon or cup to scoop dry ingredients into a measuring cup and then use the flat side of a butter knife to sweep the excess off the top. This way the dry ingredient doesn't become compressed when you scoop it out to measure.

All in Good Time

Altitude, humidity, and ingredient variations can all have an effect on cooking time. Don't be concerned if your baked goods take slightly longer or less time to cook than expected. That's why recipes give ranges of baking times. That said, if your baked goods consistently seem to be cooking slower or faster than recipes indicate, your oven calibration might be off. Invest in an oven thermometer (you can purchase one for less than $10) to be sure you are baking at the temperature you think you are.

Melting Butter Butter can be cut into chunks and melted on the stove top over medium heat, or in a microwave-safe container on low power in the microwave. Take care on the stove that you do not allow the butter to brown, and in the microwave that it does not bubble over.

Melting Chocolate The most reliable way to melt chocolate is on the stove top using a double boiler. If you don't own a double boiler, place a heat-proof bowl over a pan containing about an inch of simmering water (make sure the bottom of your bowl does not touch the water) and stir the chocolate until it melts.

Rolling Dough Before you begin rolling out dough, flour the work surface properly, the rolling pin, and, if the dough is particularly sticky, your hands. Keep a cup with a bit of extra flour next to you so you can re-flour the surface and the dough, as needed. If your recipe calls for it, make sure the dough is properly chilled before you begin. This is particularly important with pie dough and cut-out cookies.

Once your workstation and dough are ready, use the rolling pin to gently roll the dough from the inside out, pressing less hard as you get to the edges so they don't get too thin. If rolling out pie dough, lift and turn the dough as you go to ensure an even, round circle. Warm dough can be difficult to work with, so work quickly, particularly during the summer. If your dough becomes sticky and hard to handle, return it to the refrigerator for 10 to 15 minutes so it firms up again.

Separating Eggs You don't need any special tools to separate an egg easily. Simply crack the egg over a small bowl and carefully slide the yolk between the two eggshell halves until all the whites fall to the bowl beneath. Never separate eggs over the bowl containing the rest of your ingredients, because if the yolk breaks it will contaminate the mixture.

Muffins & Breads

There's nothing quite like starting your morning with a freshly baked muffin or a sweet roll straight out of the oven. In this chapter, you will find delicious sweet and savory muffins, biscuits, rolls, and more. These recipes are fantastically simple and most require little more than a whisk, a couple of bowls, and a hot oven.

Tips & Techniques

The no-fuss nature of most of these recipes makes them favorites in my kitchen. Muffins, scones, and quick breads are easier and more forgiving than many other baked goods. Still, these tips and techniques will ensure you get the best results possible.

Ingredient Temperature Pay close attention to the temperature of your ingredients. All recipes are straightforward and easy to make, but rely heavily on properly softened or chilled ingredients. Too-warm butter will make a melty, oily mess of scone dough, and you will have a hard time properly mixing butter with sugar for muffins if the butter is not at room temperature!

Correct Mixing Speaking of mixing, you will have the best success if you follow the mixing instructions closely. "Well mixed" means the ingredients are mixed until completely incorporated and smooth, while "just mixed" or "just combined" means just that. Mix only until you no longer see distinct streaks of one ingredient in the other. Some lumps are fine.

Preparing Loaf Pans A sheet of parchment paper will ensure that quick breads come out of their pans whole and perfect. To line the pans, fold a sheet of parchment in half, the curling sides facing outward, and trim it to fit lengthwise in the pan (the paper will fold over the long sides). It doesn't have to completely touch the short ends, but the closer you can get, the better. Grease the empty pan and press the parchment over the greased surface, making sure it lies flat so no batter can flow underneath. Finally, fold the tops of the paper over the sides, and trim them if they are unruly.

Testing for Doneness

Don't rely solely on visual clues when checking for doneness. These small-batch recipes may use an egg white or egg yolk only, which affects how things brown. Follow testing instructions as written.

Muffins and breads require the toothpick method: Insert a toothpick or cake tester into the center of the baked goods. If it comes out wet and crumb covered, your dish needs more oven time. If it comes out dry, with only a few crumbs, it's done!

Storing

Unless otherwise noted, baked goods keep best stored in an airtight container at room temperature. For the freshest results, cool them completely on a cooling rack and transfer to an airtight container as soon as they reach room temperature.

Solutions to Your Buttermilk Woes

Buttermilk is a troublesome (but tasty!) baking ingredient, especially in small-batch baking. It appears a lot on ingredient lists, but not so often that you necessarily keep it stocked. And, when you do buy it, you use so little that leftovers go to waste. I have solutions.

TOO MUCH BUTTERMILK? Freeze it! Buttermilk freezes fantastically. For small-batch baking, freeze ¼- to ½-cup portions in freezer bags placed flat on a baking sheet. Once solid, stack the frozen bags of buttermilk in the freezer. When ready to use, place the bag in a bowl on the counter and it will thaw in about half an hour. The buttermilk will separate a little during the freezing and thawing process; just give it a quick stir and it's good to go.

NO BUTTERMILK? No problem. While nothing quite matches the tangy taste of real buttermilk, you can make a passable substitute: To a ½-cup measuring cup, add 1½ teaspoons of freshly squeezed lemon juice and then add milk to fill the cup. Let it sit for 5 minutes and use as you would regular buttermilk.

Classic Blueberry Muffins

MAKES 4 muffins

These classic blueberry muffins are moist and delicious, and one of my favorite rainy-day breakfasts. They are quick and easy to whip up and loaded with plump, juicy blueberries. Adding the optional ¼ teaspoon of grated lemon zest gives them a bright, cheerful flavor that's guaranteed to make any morning just a little bit better.

standard
muffin tin

PREP TIME
15 minutes

COOK TIME
16 to 19 minutes

COOLING OR
CHILLING TIME
5 to 10 minutes

SHELF LIFE
2 to 3 days

3 tablespoons unsalted butter, at room temperature, plus more for greasing the muffin tin

1 teaspoon all-purpose flour, plus ⅔ cup, divided

⅓ cup fresh blueberries

¼ teaspoon baking soda

⅛ teaspoon salt

¼ cup granulated sugar, plus 1 tablespoon, divided

1 large egg white

½ teaspoon vanilla extract

3 tablespoons plain yogurt

¼ teaspoon grated lemon zest (optional)

1. Preheat the oven to 375°F.

2. Line a muffin tin with four cupcake liners, or grease the tin if it is not nonstick.

3. In a small bowl, combine 1 teaspoon of flour with the blueberries. Toss to coat and set aside. The flour coating will prevent purple streaks in your muffins.

4. In another small bowl, whisk the remaining ⅔ cup of flour, the baking soda, and salt.

5. In a medium bowl, whisk the butter and ¼ cup of sugar until smooth. If the blueberries are especially tart, add up to an additional tablespoon of sugar.

6. One at a time, add the egg white, vanilla, and yogurt, whisking well after each addition until combined.

7. Stir in the lemon zest (if using) and flour mixture just until combined.

8. Gently fold in the blueberries. Evenly divide the batter among the 4 muffin cups.

9. Bake for 16 to 19 minutes until a toothpick inserted in the center of a muffin comes out with only a few dry crumbs.

10. Cool the muffins in the tin for 5 to 10 minutes, or until cool enough to handle. Transfer to plates or place on a cooling rack to finish cooling before storing.

Substitution Tip Yogurt gives these muffins their wonderfully moist texture. Don't have any plain yogurt? Substitute flavored yogurt (just make sure it's a compatible flavor) or sour cream.

Strawberry Streusel Muffins

MAKES 4 muffins

standard
muffin tin

PREP TIME
15 minutes

COOK TIME
17 to 20 minutes

COOLING OR
CHILLING TIME
5 to 10 minutes

SHELF LIFE
2 to 3 days

There is just something about strawberries that makes everything taste better. These streusel muffins are no exception. Stuffed full of fresh strawberries and topped with crunchy brown sugar streusel, they are a sweet way to start your morning, or stash one in your work bag and look forward to a refreshing afternoon snack.

FOR THE MUFFINS

3 tablespoons unsalted butter, at
　　room temperature, plus more
　　for greasing the muffin tin

⅔ cup all-purpose flour

¼ teaspoon baking soda

⅛ teaspoon salt

⅛ teaspoon ground nutmeg

¼ cup granulated sugar

1 large egg white

½ teaspoon vanilla extract

3 tablespoons plain yogurt

⅓ cup diced fresh strawberries

FOR THE STREUSEL TOPPING

1 tablespoon all-purpose flour

1 tablespoon packed brown sugar

1 tablespoon granulated sugar

1 tablespoon unsalted cold
　　butter, diced

1. Preheat the oven to 375°F.

2. Line a muffin tin with four cupcake liners, or grease the tin if it is not nonstick.

TO MAKE THE MUFFINS

1. In a small bowl, whisk the flour, baking soda, salt, and nutmeg. Set aside.

2. In a medium bowl, whisk the butter and granulated sugar until smooth.

3. One at a time, add the egg white, vanilla, and yogurt, whisking well after each addition until combined.

4. Stir in the flour mixture just until combined.

5. Gently fold in the strawberries.

6. Fill the muffin tins just three-fourths full. (If you have a couple tablespoons of batter left over, discard it).

TO MAKE THE STREUSEL TOPPING

1. In a small bowl, mix the flour, brown sugar, and granulated sugar.

2. Add the butter and use your fingers to rub it into the mixture until rough crumbs form and the mixture clumps. Top each muffin with one-fourth of the streusel crumbles.

3. Bake for 17 to 20 minutes, or until a toothpick inserted into the center of a muffin comes out clean.

4. Cool the muffins in the tin for 5 to 10 minutes before transferring to a cooling rack. Cool completely before storing.

Ingredient Tip Nutmeg gives these muffins a delicious fresh taste, but if you don't like nutmeg in your baked goods, omit it!

mini muffin tin

PREP TIME
20 minutes

COOK TIME
10 to 13 minutes

COOLING OR
CHILLING TIME
10 minutes

SHELF LIFE
2 to 3 days

Cinnamon Swirl Vanilla—Glazed Muffin Bites

MAKES 12 mini muffins

Want a sweet cinnamon treat to start your day, but don't have the couple of hours it takes for a batch of cinnamon rolls? I have just the thing for you. These cinnamon swirl muffin bites are the perfect level of sweet and cinnamon spicy and are so cute and quick to make. The muffin batter is swirled with a generous vein of brown sugar and cinnamon, and topped with a vanilla glaze that sets and crunches as it cools. These also make a terrific teatime treat or a pick-me-up any time of day!

FOR THE MUFFINS

3 tablespoons unsalted butter, at room temperature, plus ½ tablespoon unsalted butter, melted, plus more for greasing the muffin tin

⅔ cup all-purpose flour

¼ teaspoon baking soda

⅛ teaspoon salt

2 tablespoons packed brown sugar

1 teaspoon ground cinnamon

¼ cup granulated sugar

1 large egg white

½ teaspoon vanilla extract

3 tablespoons plain yogurt

FOR THE VANILLA GLAZE

½ cup powdered sugar, sifted

1 tablespoon milk

¼ teaspoon vanilla extract

1. Preheat the oven to 375°F.

2. Grease the muffin tin if it is not nonstick.

TO MAKE THE MUFFINS

1. In a small bowl, whisk the flour, baking soda, and salt. Set aside.

2. In another small bowl, stir together the brown sugar, ½ tablespoon of melted butter, and cinnamon until well mixed. Set aside.

3. In a medium bowl, whisk 3 tablespoons of butter and the granulated sugar until well mixed.

4. One at a time, add the egg white, vanilla, and yogurt, whisking well after each addition until combined.

5. Stir in the flour mixture just until mixed.

6. With a rubber spatula, swirl the brown sugar mixture into the batter, mixing just enough to distribute it through the batter while still keeping distinct swirls of cinnamon sugar visible. Fill 12 mini muffin cups three-fourths full.

7. Bake for 10 to 13 minutes until a toothpick inserted into the center of a muffin comes out mostly clean.

8. Cool the muffins in the tin for 5 minutes before transferring to a cooling rack.

TO MAKE THE VANILLA GLAZE

In a small bowl, whisk the powdered sugar, milk, and vanilla until smooth. Dip the slightly cooled muffins in the glaze and let them sit for 5 to 10 minutes before eating.

Variation Tip The vanilla glaze over these muffins is truly decadent, but they are also fantastic plain, dusted with raw sugar, or with the streusel from the Strawberry Streusel Muffins (page 28).

standard
muffin tin

PREP TIME
15 minutes

COOK TIME
17 to 20 minutes

COOLING OR
CHILLING TIME
5 to 10 minutes

SHELF LIFE
2 to 3 days

Savory Breakfast Muffins

MAKES 4 muffins

Who says muffins have to be sweet? These savory breakfast muffins are half muffin, half biscuit, all delicious, and filled with Cheddar cheese and diced ham. You'll definitely get a few strange looks when you serve them, but they always seem to be the first thing to disappear from the brunch table.

⅔ cup all-purpose flour

¼ teaspoon baking soda

¼ teaspoon salt

Pinch cayenne pepper

3 tablespoons unsalted butter,
     at room temperature

1 tablespoon granulated sugar

1 large egg white

3 tablespoons sour cream

¼ cup shredded Cheddar cheese

¼ cup small-diced cooked ham

Favorite hot sauce, for
     seasoning (optional)

1. Preheat the oven to 375°F.

2. Line a muffin tin with four cupcake liners. (Cheese can be tough on even the most nonstick surfaces so I always make these with liners.)

3. In a small bowl, whisk the flour, baking soda, salt, and cayenne pepper.

4. In a medium bowl, whisk the butter and sugar until smooth.

5. Add the egg white and sour cream and whisk until well combined.

6. Stir in the flour mixture, mixing just until combined.

7. Fold in the Cheddar cheese and ham.

8. Evenly divide the batter among the 4 muffin cups.

9. Sprinkle 1 or 2 drops of hot sauce on the top of each muffin (if using).

10. Bake for 17 to 20 minutes until a toothpick inserted into the center of a muffin comes out clean.

11. Cool the muffins in the tin for 5 to 10 minutes and transfer to a cooling rack. Cool completely before refrigerating in an airtight container.

Variation Tip These muffins are just begging to be customized with your favorite ingredients. Add finely diced scallions or chives to the batter; switch out the ham for your favorite cooked breakfast meat; or try a sweet, fruity hot sauce for a fantastic sweet and savory combo. The options are endless.

2 mini loaf pans

PREP TIME
20 minutes

COOK TIME
25 to 30 minutes

COOLING OR
CHILLING TIME
15 minutes

SHELF LIFE
2 to 3 days

Spiced Banana Bread with Walnut Streusel

MAKES 2 mini loaves

There is no better use for overripe bananas than a batch of banana bread. This version is so good it will have you "forgetting" to eat that last banana or two in the bunch just for an excuse to make it. Generously spiced with cinnamon, nutmeg, and cloves, and topped with walnut and brown sugar streusel, it's not just another banana bread, it's the banana bread.

FOR THE BANANA BREAD

3 tablespoons unsalted butter, at room temperature, plus more for greasing the loaf pans

1 cup all-purpose flour

1½ teaspoons baking powder

¼ teaspoon salt

¼ teaspoon ground cinnamon

⅛ teaspoon ground nutmeg

⅛ teaspoon ground cloves

⅔ cup granulated sugar

1 large egg white

⅓ cup milk

½ teaspoon vanilla extract

½ cup mashed banana

FOR THE STREUSEL

2 tablespoons all-purpose flour

1 tablespoon packed brown sugar

½ teaspoon ground cinnamon

1 tablespoon unsalted butter, melted

¼ cup walnuts, roughly chopped

1. Preheat the oven to 350°F.

2. Grease the loaf pans and line them with parchment paper.

TO MAKE THE BANANA BREAD

1. In a small bowl, whisk together the flour, baking powder, salt, cinnamon, nutmeg, and cloves.

2. In a medium bowl, whisk the butter until smooth. Add the granulated sugar and whisk for 30 seconds until completely incorporated.

3. To the butter mixture, add the egg white, milk, vanilla, and banana, one at a time, whisking well after each addition until combined.

4. Stir in the flour mixture just until combined.

TO MAKE THE STREUSEL

1. In a small bowl, mix the flour, brown sugar, and cinnamon. Add the butter, stirring until the mixture begins to clump and the butter is incorporated. Stir in the walnuts.

2. Evenly divide the batter between the prepared pans. Top each with half of the streusel.

3. Bake for 25 to 30 minutes until a toothpick inserted into the center of the loaves comes out clean.

4. Cool the loaves in the pans for 15 minutes before slicing or transferring to a rack. Cool completely before storing.

Variation Tip Don't like nuts? Leave them out of the streusel. Love nuts? Add another ¼ cup to the batter. Like your banana bread with less spice? Omit the nutmeg and cloves for a milder flavor.

Cream Cheese Pumpkin Bread

MAKES 2 mini loaves

2 mini loaf pans

PREP TIME
20 minutes

COOK TIME
30 to 35 minutes

COOLING OR
CHILLING TIME
15 minutes

SHELF LIFE
2 to 3 days

This bread is fall in a loaf pan—moist, perfectly spiced pumpkin bread with a layer of rich cream cheese through the center. One bite and you'll be dreaming of crisp fall days, pumpkin spice lattes, and big slouchy sweaters. Oh, that it could always be the first few weeks of October!

Butter or shortening, for greasing
   the loaf pans

¾ cup all-purpose flour

1½ teaspoons baking powder

½ teaspoon ground cinnamon

¼ teaspoon salt

⅛ teaspoon ground cloves

⅛ teaspoon ground nutmeg

1 large egg

¾ cup granulated sugar

½ cup pumpkin purée

¼ cup canola oil

4 ounces cream cheese,
   at room temperature

1 large egg yolk

1 teaspoon vanilla extract

½ cup powdered sugar

1. Preheat the oven to 350°F.

2. Grease the loaf pans and line them with parchment paper.

3. In a small bowl, mix the flour, baking powder, cinnamon, salt, cloves, and nutmeg. Set aside.

4. In a medium bowl, whisk together the egg, granulated sugar, pumpkin, and canola oil until smooth.

5. Stir in the flour mixture just until combined.

6. In another medium bowl, whisk the cream cheese, egg yolk, and vanilla until smooth. Whisk in the powdered sugar until well combined.

7. Spoon about one-fourth of the pumpkin batter into the bottom of each loaf pan. Top each with half of the cream cheese mixture. With a plastic spatula, gently spread the cream cheese over the batter. Cover each with half of the remaining pumpkin batter.

8. Bake for 30 to 35 minutes. The cream cheese layer will make the toothpick method unreliable when testing for doneness, so bake until the top of the bread springs (slowly) back when gently pressed.

9. Cool the loaves in the pans for 15 minutes before serving or transferring to a rack to finish cooling before storing. Wrap leftovers and refrigerate.

Variation Tip Make Nutella pumpkin bread by leaving out the cream cheese mixture and substituting ¼ cup of Nutella. Melt the Nutella in the microwave in 20- to 30-second bursts on high, stirring in between, until easily pourable. Evenly divide the pumpkin mixture between the two pans and pour the Nutella over the top. With a knife, swirl the Nutella in a serpentine pattern, then drag the knife once down the center of the mixture. Bake as directed.

Zucchini Bread

MAKES 2 mini loaves

2 mini loaf pans

PREP TIME
15 minutes

COOK TIME
25 to 30 minutes

COOLING OR
CHILLING TIME
10 minutes

SHELF LIFE
2 to 3 days

During summer, my mom would make loaves of this zucchini bread and the smell of cloves and cinnamon would fill the house. This recipe is on a battered index card in her kitchen, a hand-me-down from a beloved neighbor.

Butter or shortening, for greasing the loaf pans

1 cup all-purpose flour

1½ teaspoons baking powder

½ teaspoon ground cinnamon

¼ teaspoon ground cloves

¼ teaspoon salt

⅛ teaspoon ground nutmeg

1 large egg

½ cup granulated sugar

⅓ cup vegetable oil

½ teaspoon vanilla extract

¾ cup grated zucchini

¼ cup chopped walnuts

1. Preheat the oven to 350°F.

2. Grease the loaf pans and line them with parchment paper.

3. In a small bowl, mix the flour, baking powder, cinnamon, cloves, salt, and nutmeg. Set aside.

4. In a medium bowl, whisk the egg, sugar, vegetable oil, and vanilla until well combined.

5. Stir in the flour mixture just until combined.

6. Fold in the zucchini and walnuts. Evenly divide the batter between the prepared loaf pans.

7. Bake for 25 to 30 minutes until a toothpick inserted into the center of the loaves comes out clean.

8. Cool the loaves in the pans for 10 minutes until cool enough to handle, then transfer to a cooling rack, or serve. Cool completely before storing.

Cooking Tip Quick breads freeze very well. Wrap tightly in aluminum foil and store in an airtight freezer bag. To serve, unwrap and reheat slices in the microwave, or allow the entire loaf to come to room temperature on a cooling rack so the bottom doesn't become soggy.

Basic Roll Dough Cinnamon Rolls

MAKES 4 cinnamon rolls

7-by-7-inch
square baking dish

PREP TIME
20 minutes

COOK TIME
12 to 17 minutes

COOLING,
CHILLING, AND
RISING TIME
1 hour, 45 minutes

SHELF LIFE
2 to 3 days

I have a version of these cinnamon rolls on my site, Baking Mischief, and they are one of the most popular recipes on the blog, for good reason. They are delicious, easy, and the most perfectly ooey gooey way to start (or finish!) your day. And the cream cheese frosting? It will make your toes curl with delight.

FOR THE BASIC ROLL DOUGH

⅓ cup warm milk (105°F to 115°F)

1 teaspoon active dry yeast

2 tablespoons unsalted butter, melted, plus more for greasing the baking dish

2 tablespoons granulated sugar

1 large egg yolk

¼ teaspoon salt

1¼ cups all-purpose flour, plus more for flouring the work surface and the rolling pin

Cooking spray

FOR THE FILLING

⅓ cup packed brown sugar

1 teaspoon ground cinnamon

2 tablespoons unsalted butter, at room temperature

FOR THE CREAM CHEESE FROSTING

3 ounces cream cheese, at room temperature

3 tablespoons unsalted butter, at room temperature

1 cup powdered sugar

½ teaspoon vanilla extract

Pinch salt

TO MAKE THE BASIC ROLL DOUGH

1. In a small bowl or cup, stir together the warm milk and yeast. Set aside for 10 to 15 minutes until the top of the milk looks foamy. If the mixture doesn't become foamy, the yeast might be old. Try a new packet. Or you might have killed the yeast if the milk was too hot. Try again with milk that is just lukewarm.

2. In a medium bowl, whisk the butter, granulated sugar, egg yolk, and salt.

3. Whisk in the yeast mixture.

CONTINUED

4. Stir in the flour, one-third at a time, until a thick dough forms and begins to pull away from the sides of the bowl. If the dough reaches this consistency before you have added all the flour, stop. That's fine!

5. Turn out the dough onto a well-floured work surface. Knead for 2 to 3 minutes, adding more flour as necessary to prevent sticking, until the dough is smooth and can be shaped into a tidy ball.

6. Spray a large bowl with cooking spray and place the dough inside. Cover with a clean kitchen towel and place it in a warm spot free of drafts. Let the dough rise for an hour, or until doubled in size.

7. Lightly flour your work surface again (you will need about a 24-by-12-inch workspace), and a rolling pin. Gently squeeze and stretch the dough into an oblong shape (make a snake) about 12 inches long, being careful not to rip it. Lay the dough on the prepared surface and roll it out to about 5 inches by 15 inches, gently manipulating the edges so you have a fairly even rectangle.

8. Grease the baking dish.

TO MAKE THE FILLING

1. In a small bowl, mix the brown sugar and cinnamon.

2. Spread the butter over the dough. Sprinkle the brown sugar mixture over it.

3. From one of the short sides, roll the dough as tightly and neatly as possible.

4. Using plain dental floss or a serrated knife, cut the rolled dough into 4 equal parts and transfer them to the prepared dish. Cover and let rise for 30 minutes in a warm place.

5. Preheat the oven to 400°F.

6. Bake the rolls for 12 to 17 minutes until the tops are golden and the center (where all 4 rolls meet) is no longer doughy. Let cool slightly before frosting. Cover and refrigerate any leftover rolls.

TO MAKE THE CREAM CHEESE FROSTING

In a medium bowl, whisk the cream cheese, butter, powdered sugar, vanilla, and salt. Spread the frosting over the warm cinnamon rolls.

Cooking Tip To make these rolls overnight, complete the recipe through to cutting the rolls and placing them in the baking dish. Cover them tightly with plastic wrap and refrigerate overnight, or up to 24 hours. The next morning, remove the plastic wrap and place the dish into a cold oven. Bake at 400° for 16 to 24 minutes until the tops are golden.

The frosting can also be prepared the night before. Refrigerate it in an airtight container and remove it 30 minutes before you begin to bake the rolls so it has time to warm up. The frosting will heat up quickly when placed on the warm rolls, so don't worry if it has not reached room temperature by the time the rolls have finished baking.

Strawberry Rolls with Cream Cheese Glaze

7-by-7-inch
square baking dish

PREP TIME
20 minutes

COOK TIME
20 to 30 minutes

COOLING,
CHILLING, AND
RISING TIME
1 hour, 35 minutes

SHELF LIFE
2 to 3 days

MAKES 4 rolls

These rolls are sure to delight any strawberry lover. The filling, made with fresh fruit, is quick and easy, and the cream cheese glaze gives the perfect kiss of tangy sweetness to the already stunning rolls.

FOR THE ROLLS

1 recipe Basic Roll Dough (page 39)

Butter or shortening, for greasing
   the baking dish

FOR THE FILLING

2 cups diced fresh strawberries

½ cup granulated sugar

2 tablespoons cornstarch

1 tablespoon unsalted butter, melted

FOR THE CREAM CHEESE GLAZE

2 ounces cream cheese,
   at room temperature

1 tablespoon unsalted butter,
   at room temperature

½ cup powdered sugar

1 tablespoon milk or heavy (whipping)
   cream, plus more as needed

¼ teaspoon vanilla extract

Pinch salt

TO MAKE THE ROLLS

1. Prepare the Basic Roll Dough recipe. When the dough begins its first rise, make the filling.

2. Grease the baking dish.

TO MAKE THE FILLING

1. In a 2-quart saucepan over medium heat, combine the strawberries, granulated sugar, and cornstarch. Bring the mixture to a simmer and cook, stirring occasionally, for about 2 minutes until thick and syrupy. Remove from the heat and let cool for at least 30 minutes before using.

2. Once the roll dough is prepared and rolled out and the strawberry filling has cooled, use a pastry brush to spread a thin layer of melted butter over the dough (you may not need all of it).

3. Spread the strawberry filling over the butter.

4. From one of the short sides, roll the dough as tightly and neatly as possible. Some strawberry filling will squeeze out of the sides. Don't worry! With a serrated knife, gently cut the dough into 4 even pieces. With a metal spatula to help support the dough and hold in the filling, transfer them to the pre-pared dish. Cover and let the rolls rise for 30 minutes in a warm place.

5. Preheat the oven to 375°F.

6. Bake the rolls for 20 to 30 minutes until golden and the center (where all 4 rolls meet) no longer seems doughy. Keep a close eye on the rolls during the second half of the cooking time. If they begin to brown too quickly and the inside of the dough still seems undercooked, cover the rolls with aluminum foil for the remainder of the cooking time.

7. Cool for at least 5 minutes before making the glaze. Leftovers should be tightly covered and refrigerated.

TO MAKE THE CREAM CHEESE GLAZE

In a medium bowl, whisk the cream cheese, butter, powdered sugar, milk, vanilla, and salt. Add more milk by the teaspoon as needed to get the desired consistency for a pourable glaze. Spoon the glaze over the warm rolls.

Cooking Tip Don't be alarmed if the rolls seem to be taking longer than expected to cook. Different levels of liquid in the fruit can make them take more or less time than the recipe suggests. If you are unsure whether the rolls are done, take two forks and gently separate the rolls where they meet. The dough will be quite moist, but it should not look raw.

Pizza Rolls

MAKES 4 rolls

7-by-7-inch
square baking dish

PREP TIME
20 minutes

COOK TIME
45 to 60 minutes

COOLING,
CHILLING, AND
RISING TIME
1 hour, 35 minutes

SHELF LIFE
2 to 3 days

So often in life, we ask "Why?" when we could be asking "Why not?" Why pizza rolls? Why not pizza rolls? They are gooey, cheesy, and downright tasty. Plus they are fun to make and pretty to look at. Homemade pizza sauce, mozzarella, Parmesan, and pepperoni, all wrapped up in rolls and baked until golden? Sounds like tonight's pizza night.

FOR THE ROLLS

1 recipe Basic Roll Dough (page 39)

FOR THE PIZZA SAUCE

1 (15-ounce) can whole tomatoes

2 tablespoons extra-virgin olive oil

2 large garlic cloves, pressed
    or minced

4 large fresh basil leaves, thinly sliced

¼ teaspoon granulated sugar

FOR THE FILLING

Butter or shortening, for greasing
    the baking dish

16 pepperoni slices, quartered

½ cup shredded mozzarella cheese

¼ cup shredded Parmesan cheese

TO MAKE THE ROLLS

Prepare the Basic Roll Dough recipe. When the dough begins its first rise, make the pizza sauce.

TO MAKE THE PIZZA SAUCE

1. In a food processor or blender, or with an immersion blender, purée the tomatoes (or take a pair of scissors and chop the tomatoes to little bits in the can). It's okay if some chunks remain.

2. In a large saucepan over medium heat (using a large saucepan cuts down on cooking time and reduces sauce splatter), heat the olive oil and garlic for about 1 minute until golden.

3. Pour in the puréed tomatoes.

4. Stir in the basil and sugar. Bring to a simmer and cook, stirring occasionally, for 20 to 25 minutes until the sauce thickens and reduces to about ¾ cup. Remove from the heat and set aside. Let the sauce cool.

TO MAKE THE FILLING

1. Grease the baking dish and set aside.

2. In a medium skillet over medium heat, cook the pepperoni pieces for 2 to 4 minutes, depending on the thickness of the slices, just until they begin to curl and look cooked. Do not cook until crispy—you won't be able to roll them in your rolls if they are too rigid. Transfer the pepperoni to a paper towel-lined plate and set aside.

3. Preheat the oven to 375°F.

4. Once the dough is prepared and rolled out, spread the sauce over it.

5. Top with the mozzarella cheese and pepperoni slices. From one of the short sides, roll the dough as tightly and neatly as possible. With a serrated knife, gently cut the dough into 4 equal pieces. Transfer them to the prepared dish. Cover and let rise for 30 minutes in a warm place.

6. Sprinkle the Parmesan over the top of the rolls and bake for 20 to 30 minutes until the tops are golden and the center (where all 4 rolls meet) no longer seems doughy. If the tops brown too quickly, cover the baking dish with aluminum foil.

7. Cool for 5 minutes before serving. Cover and refrigerate any leftovers.

Variation Tip Add your favorite pizza toppings—olives, onions, bell peppers, etc.—to these rolls. Finely dice the additions and give the crunchy ones a quick sauté to reduce their raw bite before sprinkling them over the cheese.

Orange–Chocolate Chip Scones with Orange Glaze

baking sheet

PREP TIME
15 minutes

COOK TIME
10 to 12 minutes

COOLING OR
CHILLING TIME
10 minutes

SHELF LIFE
1 to 2 days

MAKES 4 scones

These scones come together in minutes and bake up big and beautiful. I'm a firm believer in the more chocolate the better, so they are absolutely packed full of mini chocolate chips. A bit of orange zest in the dough gives them a fresh citrus spark and the finishing drizzle of a quick orange glaze makes them downright unforgettable.

FOR THE SCONES

2 tablespoons cold unsalted butter, cut into ½-inch pieces, plus more for greasing the baking sheet

1 cup all-purpose flour, plus more for flouring the work surface

1 tablespoon granulated sugar

1 teaspoon baking powder

¼ teaspoon baking soda

⅛ teaspoon salt

½ cup mini semisweet chocolate chips

½ teaspoon grated orange zest

⅓ cup buttermilk

FOR THE ORANGE GLAZE

¼ cup powdered sugar

1 teaspoon milk

¼ teaspoon grated orange zest

1. Preheat the oven to 450°F.

2. Lightly grease a baking sheet.

TO MAKE THE SCONES

1. In a medium bowl, mix the flour, granulated sugar, baking powder, baking soda, and salt.

2. With a pastry blender, two knives, or your fingers, cut the butter into the flour mixture until no pieces larger than a pea remain.

3. Stir in the chocolate chips and orange zest.

4. Pour in the buttermilk, mixing with a rubber spatula until a thick, messy dough forms. Turn out the dough onto a well-floured surface and knead 4 or 5 times just until it comes together and can be formed into a ball. Press the dough out into a 6-inch disk. With a knife or bench scraper, cut the disk into quarters. Transfer the scones to the prepared baking sheet and bake for 10 to 12 minutes until the scones are just lightly golden.

5. Cool the scones on the baking sheet for at least 10 minutes before glazing.

TO MAKE THE ORANGE GLAZE

In a small bowl, stir together the powdered sugar, milk, and orange zest. Drizzle over the cooled scones. For a thinner glaze, add milk by the ¼ teaspoon until it reaches the desired consistency.

Ingredient Tip Want plain chocolate chip scones? Omit the orange zest in both the scones and the glaze. Add ½ teaspoon of vanilla extract to the scone dough and ¼ teaspoon vanilla extract to the glaze.

Tammy's Bacon Scones with Maple Glaze

baking sheet

PREP TIME
20 minutes

COOK TIME
20 to 25 minutes

COOLING OR
CHILLING TIME
10 minutes

SHELF LIFE
1 to 2 days

MAKES 4 scones

The addictive nature of these scones might sneak up on you, even if you are a person who doesn't normally appreciate sweet and savory combinations. At first bite, you get a burst of sweet maple glaze, but it doesn't take long before the salty, smoky taste of bacon comes out to play, and suddenly there's a maple bacon party going on in your mouth and you're not sure you ever want it to stop. These scones are named after my little sister who scoffed and wrinkled her nose the first time I made them for her, then ate every single one.

FOR THE SCONES

2 tablespoons cold unsalted butter, cut into ½-inch pieces, plus more for greasing the baking sheet

3 slices bacon

1 cup all-purpose flour, plus more for flouring the work surface

1 tablespoon granulated sugar

1 teaspoon baking powder

¼ teaspoon baking soda

⅛ teaspoon salt

⅓ cup buttermilk

FOR THE MAPLE GLAZE

¼ cup powdered sugar

1 teaspoon milk

⅛ teaspoon maple extract

1. Preheat the oven to 450°F.

2. Lightly grease a baking sheet.

TO MAKE THE SCONES

1. Using your preferred method, cook the bacon until crisp. When cool enough to handle, crumble or chop it into ¼-inch pieces and set aside.

2. In a medium bowl, mix the flour, granulated sugar, baking powder, baking soda, and salt.

3. With a pastry blender, two knives, or your fingers, cut the butter into the flour mixture until no pieces larger than a pea remain. Stir in two-thirds of the bacon, reserving the rest for a topping.

4. Stir in the buttermilk until a thick dough forms. Turn out the dough onto a well-floured surface and knead 4 or 5 times, just until the dough comes together and can be formed into a ball. Press the dough out into a 6-inch disk. With a knife or bench scraper, cut the disk into quarters. Transfer the scones to the prepared baking sheet and bake for 10 to 12 minutes until the scones are just lightly golden.

5. Cool the scones on the baking sheet for 10 minutes before glazing.

TO MAKE THE MAPLE GLAZE

In a small bowl, whisk the powdered sugar, milk, and maple extract until smooth. Drizzle over the cooled scones. Sprinkle the reserved bacon pieces on top and serve.

Cooking Tip My favorite no-fuss way to cook bacon is to bake it in the oven for 10 to 15 minutes at 400°F on a baking rack over an aluminum foil–covered baking sheet. This makes cleanup quick and easy and means you don't have to stand over the bacon while it cooks.

Herb and Cheese Savory Scones

baking sheet

PREP TIME
15 minutes

COOK TIME
10 to 12 minutes

COOLING OR
CHILLING TIME
5 minutes

SHELF LIFE
1 to 2 days

MAKES 4 scones

Few things in life can't be improved by a handful of cheese and a sprinkling of fresh herbs, and these scones, with their tangy buttermilk base, come out particularly well. They make a great grab-and-go breakfast, but are also superb with a warm bowl of soup on a blustery day.

2 tablespoons cold unsalted butter, cut into ½-inch pieces, plus more for greasing the baking sheet

1 cup all-purpose flour, plus more for flouring the work surface

1 teaspoon granulated sugar

1 teaspoon baking powder

¼ teaspoon baking soda

⅛ teaspoon salt

¼ cup shredded sharp Cheddar cheese

½ teaspoon minced fresh chives

⅓ cup buttermilk

1. Preheat the oven to 450°F.

2. Lightly grease a baking sheet.

3. In a medium bowl, whisk the flour, sugar, baking powder, baking soda, and salt.

4. With a pastry blender, two knives, or your fingers, cut the butter into the flour mixture until no pieces larger than a pea remain.

5. Stir in the Cheddar cheese and chives.

6. Slowly mix in the buttermilk, stirring just until a thick dough forms. Turn out the dough onto a well-floured work surface and knead about 5 times until the dough starts to come together. Form a ball and press the dough out into a ½-inch-thick disk. With a knife or bench scraper, cut the disk into quarters. Transfer the scones to the prepared baking sheet and bake for 10 to 12 minutes until lightly browned.

7. Cool the scones on the sheet for at least 5 minutes before serving. Cool completely before storing.

Substitution Tip Don't have chives or Cheddar on hand? Substitute your favorite cheese and fresh herbs! Robust cheeses that can be easily grated work best, and you can use up to 2 teaspoons of your favorite fresh herbs (minced), depending on the strength of their flavor.

Honey Buttermilk Biscuits

baking sheet

PREP TIME
10 minutes

COOK TIME
10 to 12 minutes

COOLING OR
CHILLING TIME
5 minutes

SHELF LIFE
2 to 3 days

MAKES 4 biscuits

Homemade biscuits can make even the most lackluster weeknight dinner feel like a feast. These biscuits are soft, flaky, and buttery—with just a hint of honey sweetness. While optional, the egg wash will turn your biscuits beautiful, shiny, and golden.

No time? No problem. They whip up fast and easily, and freeze well for those nights when you know there will be no time for down-home cooking. See the Cooking Tip for freezing instructions.

FOR THE BISCUITS

4 tablespoons cold unsalted butter, cubed, plus more for greasing the baking sheet

1 cup all-purpose flour, plus more for flouring the work surface

1 teaspoon baking powder

¼ teaspoon baking soda

¼ teaspoon salt

⅓ cup buttermilk

1 tablespoon honey

FOR THE EGG WASH (OPTIONAL)

1 large egg

1 tablespoon milk

1. Preheat the oven to 425°F.

2. Lightly grease a baking sheet.

TO MAKE THE BISCUITS

1. In a medium bowl, stir together the flour, baking powder, baking soda, and salt.

2. With a pastry blender, two knives, or your fingers, cut the butter into the flour mixture until no pieces larger than a pea remain.

3. Stir in the buttermilk and honey until a thick, messy dough forms. Turn out the dough onto a well-floured surface and knead 10 times until the dough is no longer sticky. Pat the dough out to ½-inch thickness. With a 3-inch biscuit cutter (or cup), cut out 4 biscuits. Transfer the biscuits to the prepared baking sheet.

TO MAKE THE EGG WASH (IF USING)

1. In a small bowl, whisk the egg and milk and brush the egg wash over the biscuits.

2. Bake for 10 to 12 minutes until golden.

3. Cool the biscuits for 5 minutes on the baking sheet before serving.

Cooking Tip This biscuit dough is perfect for freezing. Prepare the dough and cut out the biscuits, but instead of baking them, place them on a plate in the freezer. Once the dough has frozen solid, store the biscuits in a freezer bag. If you plan to freeze the biscuits for more than a week, wrap them individually in plastic wrap or aluminum foil before putting them in the bag, to ensure they stay fresh. To bake, brush with the egg wash (if using) and bake at the normal temperature for 1 to 3 minutes longer. No need to thaw.

baking sheet

PREP TIME
20 minutes

COOK TIME
20 to 25 minutes

COOLING OR
CHILLING TIME
5 minutes

SHELF LIFE
2 to 3 days

Cheesy Bacon Biscuits

MAKES 4 biscuits

How do you improve warm, buttery buttermilk biscuits, one of the greatest comfort foods? You add cheese and bacon! Okay, these biscuits are supremely indulgent, but that's the beauty of small-batch baking: You have built-in portion control!

FOR THE BISCUITS

4 tablespoons cold unsalted
   butter, cubed, plus more for
   greasing the baking sheet

3 slices bacon

1 cup all-purpose flour, plus more
   for flouring the work surface

1 teaspoon baking powder

¼ teaspoon baking soda

¼ teaspoon salt

¼ cup shredded Cheddar cheese

⅓ cup buttermilk

FOR THE EGG WASH (OPTIONAL)

1 large egg

1 tablespoon milk

1. Preheat the oven to 425°F.

2. Lightly grease a baking sheet.

TO MAKE THE BISCUITS

1. Using your preferred method, cook the bacon until crisp. When cool enough to handle, crumble or chop and set aside.

2. In a small bowl, whisk the flour, baking powder, baking soda, and salt.

3. With a pastry blender, two knives, or your fingers, cut the butter into the flour mixture until no pieces larger than a pea remain.

4. Stir in the Cheddar cheese and bacon pieces.

5. Slowly mix in the buttermilk, stirring until a thick, sticky dough forms. Turn out the dough onto a well-floured surface. Knead it a few times until the dough is no longer sticky. Press the dough out to ½-inch thickness. With a 3-inch biscuit cutter (or a glass), cut out 4 biscuits, combining the scraps and re-pressing the dough, if necessary.

TO MAKE THE EGG WASH (IF USING)

1. In a small bowl, whisk the egg and milk and then brush lightly over the biscuits. Transfer the biscuits to the prepared baking sheet.

2. Bake for 10 to 12 minutes until lightly golden.

3. Cool the biscuits on the baking sheet for 5 minutes before serving.

Cooking Tip Not sure if your biscuits are done? With a fork or spatula, gently tip one over and look at the bottom. If the bottom is nicely browned, it's time to take them out of the oven.

CHAPTER THREE

Cakes & Cupcakes

Whether you need a cake to celebrate a special event or just a sweet treat to celebrate how awesome you are, there's a cake or cupcake for every occasion in this chapter. From the tall and beautiful Strawberry Buttercream Layer Cake (page 76) to the throw it in the oven and forget about it Death by Chocolate Sheet Cake (page 79), you're sure to find something to love.

Tips & Techniques

Producing the perfect cake is as much about how you use your ingredients as it is about which ingredients you select. Correctly creaming butter and sugar, choosing the right mixer, and properly cooling cakes and cupcakes make all the difference.

Creaming Butter and Sugar Properly creamed butter and sugar is key to cakes with the best texture. Creaming whips air into the mixture, creating a light, fluffy cake with a tender crumb. To start, you need butter at the right temperature—room temperature. It should be softened, not melted. When you press your finger into the butter, it should give but mostly hold its shape. Whisk the butter and sugar vigorously for at least 1 minute until lighter in color and fluffy, with no butter chunks remaining.

On Electric Mixers You can make the recipes in this chapter with a whisk and elbow grease, but I call for a handheld electric mixer for some because, for the best texture, they require mixing times of 2 minutes or more. If you don't have a mixer, you can purchase a quality one for less than $40—or you can mix these recipes by hand. Electric mixers are more powerful than an arm, so you may need to whisk longer than the recommended time to achieve the texture described.

Cooling The cakes and cupcakes start cooling in their pans, but use a cooling rack right away. Transfer the pans directly from the oven to the cooling rack. This allows air to circulate around the top and bottom for faster, more even cooling.

Testing for Doneness

Again, we'll use the toothpick method to determine doneness. Cakes and cupcakes are more temperamental than muffins—do not open the oven until the end of the baking time. And don't test until the tops are domed and look set. Once the tops look set, insert a toothpick (or cake tester) into the center of the cake. If it comes out clean or with a few dry crumbs, it's ready. If it comes out shiny and wet, cook it a bit longer.

Storing

Unless otherwise noted, these recipes can be stored at room temperature in an airtight container or covered in plastic wrap. The cakes frosted with buttercream are safe to store on the counter, but in warmer months it's better to refrigerate them, as the frosting won't hold up well in the heat.

Piping the Frosting

The quickest way to look like a cupcake master is to learn how to pipe frosting. You will need:

- COUPLER
- LARGE STAR TIP
- PIPING BAGS

For big, classic swirls of frosting, start from the outside edge of the cupcake and slowly spiral in, building a mountain of frosting as you do so. If you want rose-top cupcakes, start with the tip in the center of the cupcake and spiral out.

If you don't have access to a piping set, use a disposable plastic bag with a bottom corner snipped off for smooth and billowy swirls.

And one more tip: The easiest way to fill a piping bag with frosting is to set it inside a tall cup and fold the bag over the rim so the cup holds the bag wide open while you add the frosting.

Chocolate Cupcakes with Chocolate Espresso Buttercream

standard
muffin tin

PREP TIME
15 minutes

COOK TIME
16 to 19 minutes

COOLING OR
CHILLING TIME
25 minutes

SHELF LIFE
3 to 4 days

MAKES 4 cupcakes

A good chocolate cupcake can make any occasion seem like a party, and these chocolate cupcakes are more than good; they are spectacular. Made with melted chocolate and freshly brewed coffee, their chocolate flavor is delicious. Pipe on some quick espresso buttercream, and you have one tasty afternoon treat on your hands.

FOR THE CUPCAKES

2 tablespoons unsalted butter

2 tablespoons chopped
    semisweet chocolate

1½ teaspoons vegetable oil

¼ cup all-purpose flour

2 tablespoons unsweetened natural
    cocoa powder, sifted

½ teaspoon baking powder

⅛ teaspoon salt

¼ cup granulated sugar

1 large egg yolk, at room temperature

¼ teaspoon vanilla extract

2 tablespoons milk

2 tablespoons hot coffee

**FOR THE CHOCOLATE
ESPRESSO BUTTERCREAM**

4 tablespoons unsalted butter,
    at room temperature

1 cup powdered sugar, sifted

1 teaspoon unsweetened natural
    cocoa powder

½ teaspoon instant espresso powder

1 to 2 tablespoons heavy (whipping)
    cream (optional)

1. Preheat the oven to 350°F.

2. Line the muffin tin with four cupcake liners.

TO MAKE THE CUPCAKES

1. In a small, microwave-safe bowl, microwave the butter until it's mostly melted. Add the semisweet chocolate and vegetable oil and microwave in 15-second bursts on high, stirring after each, until the chocolate is completely melted. Stir and set aside to cool.

2. In a small bowl, whisk the flour, cocoa powder, baking powder, and salt.

3. In a medium bowl, whisk the granulated sugar, egg yolk, and vanilla.

4. Whisk in the cooled chocolate (it will scramble the egg if left uncooled), until well combined.

5. Stir in the flour mixture, mixing just until combined.

6. Whisk in the milk and coffee until smooth. The batter will be thin. Pour the batter into the prepared tin, filling the cupcake liners just under three-fourths full. If you have leftover batter, discard it.

7. Bake for 16 to 19 minutes until a toothpick inserted into a cupcake center comes out clean.

8. Cool the cupcakes in the tin for 10 minutes before transferring them to a cooling rack. Cool completely, for about 15 minutes, before making the buttercream.

TO MAKE THE CHOCOLATE ESPRESSO BUTTERCREAM

In a medium bowl, whisk the butter, powdered sugar, cocoa powder, and espresso powder until smooth, light, and fluffy. If you want a thinner frosting, whisk in the cream (if using) until the frosting reaches the desired consistency. Transfer to a piping bag and pipe on big, beautiful swirls.

Ingredient Tip The coffee in these cupcakes enhances the chocolate flavor. Unless you are very sensitive to coffee, you won't notice it at all. If you want to use a different frosting and are worried about the coffee flavor, use hot water instead.

standard
muffin tin

PREP TIME
20 minutes

COOK TIME
16 to 19 minutes

COOLING OR
CHILLING TIME
25 minutes

SHELF LIFE
3 to 4 days

Chocolate Cupcakes with Candy Cane Buttercream

MAKES 4 cupcakes

Peppermint buttercream in a sweet red-and-white candy cane swirl is a fun and festive way to frost your chocolate cupcakes this winter. You don't need to buy special piping equipment. You can use the piping tools you already own or create a makeshift piping bag out of a handful of plastic bags. The cupcakes will be a cute holiday treat either way.

1 recipe (4 cupcakes) Chocolate
    Cupcakes (page 60), cooled
    completely
4 tablespoons unsalted butter, at
    room temperature

1 cup powdered sugar
⅛ teaspoon peppermint extract
Red food coloring, for coloring
    the frosting

1. In a medium bowl, whisk the butter, powdered sugar, and peppermint extract until smooth. Transfer half of the frosting to another bowl.

2. A drop at a time, whisk red food coloring into one of the bowls until the frosting turns red.

3. Drape two piping bags open over two cups and fill one bag with white frosting and one with red. Fit the third piping bag with the piping tip. Squeeze the frosting-filled bags together and slip them into the third bag. Remove them, snip the tips off both bags of frosting, and place them back into the third bag, lining them up so they sit evenly at the bottom.

4. If using plastic bags, place both frosting-filled plastic bags into a third and position them so the bags sit together in one corner. Squeeze the frosting down so it is gathered down at the point of the bags and snip the edge off all three at once.

5. Starting on the outside edge of the cooled cupcakes, pipe swirls of frosting onto each and enjoy!

Ingredient Tip For the darkest, most vibrant red buttercream, use gel food coloring, which you can find online or at craft and baking stores. Because it is more concentrated than liquid food coloring, you can get brighter colors without thinning the frosting or getting a food coloring taste.

standard
muffin tin

PREP TIME
15 minutes

COOK TIME
16 to 20 minutes

COOLING OR
CHILLING TIME
30 minutes

SHELF LIFE
3 to 4 days

White Confetti Cupcakes with Whipped Vanilla Buttercream

MAKES 4 cupcakes

A generous splash of buttermilk in the batter makes these confetti cupcakes incredibly moist and rich—no dry cupcakes allowed around here. Top them off with whipped vanilla buttercream with just a hint of almond extract and they will be the star of any party they happen upon.

FOR THE CUPCAKES

½ cups all-purpose flour

¼ teaspoon baking soda

⅛ teaspoon salt

⅓ cup granulated sugar

4 tablespoons unsalted butter,
   at room temperature

1 large egg white

½ teaspoon vanilla extract

3 tablespoons buttermilk

2 tablespoons sprinkles
   (see Ingredient Tip)

FOR THE WHIPPED VANILLA BUTTERCREAM

1 tablespoon unsalted butter,
   at room temperature

½ cup powdered sugar, sifted

1 tablespoon heavy (whipping) cream

2 or 3 drops almond extract

Pinch salt

Sprinkles, for topping

1. Preheat the oven to 350°F.

2. Line a muffin tin with four cupcake liners.

TO MAKE THE CUPCAKES

1. In a small bowl, whisk the flour, baking soda, and salt.

2. In a medium bowl, cream together the granulated sugar and butter until light and fluffy.

3. Whisk in the egg white and vanilla until well combined.

4. Whisk in the buttermilk until smooth.

5. Stir in the flour mixture just until combined and fold in the sprinkles. Fill the cupcake liners just two-thirds full. Do not overfill.

6. Bake for 16 to 20 minutes until a toothpick inserted into the center of a cupcake comes out clean.

7. Cool the cupcakes in the tin for 10 minutes before transferring to a cooling rack to cool completely, about 20 minutes.

TO MAKE THE WHIPPED VANILLA BUTTERCREAM

In a medium bowl, use an electric mixer to beat the butter, powdered sugar, heavy cream, almond extract, and salt until smooth. Taste the frosting and add more almond extract, if desired. Beat at high speed for 4 to 5 minutes until very light and fluffy. Pipe onto completely cooled cupcakes and top with sprinkles.

Ingredient Tip The best sprinkles for confetti cupcakes are the softer, long, thin, colorful sprinkles, often sold as "jimmies." They give the cupcakes distinct bursts of color without bleeding into and streaking the batter the way some other sprinkles do.

Peanut Butter Chocolate Surprise Cupcakes

standard
muffin tin

PREP TIME
15 minutes

COOK TIME
16 to 19 minutes

COOLING OR
CHILLING TIME
30 minutes

SHELF LIFE
2 to 3 days

MAKES 4 cupcakes

Peanut butter frosting on top and rich peanut butter cupcakes on the bottom. But what's this? Plot twist! There's a melty chocolate center. You're going to want a big glass of milk to go with these cupcakes.

FOR THE CUPCAKES

⅓ cup all-purpose flour

½ teaspoon baking powder

⅛ teaspoon salt

⅓ cup packed brown sugar

¼ cup creamy peanut butter

2 tablespoons unsalted butter,
    at room temperature

1 large egg white

1 teaspoon vanilla extract

2 tablespoons milk

2 tablespoons semisweet
    chocolate chips

FOR THE BROWN SUGAR–PEANUT BUTTER FROSTING

¼ cup creamy peanut butter

3 tablespoons powdered sugar

2 tablespoons packed brown sugar

2 tablespoons heavy
    (whipping) cream

1 tablespoon unsalted butter,
    at room temperature

¼ teaspoon vanilla extract

1. Preheat the oven to 350°F.

2. Line a muffin tin with four cupcake liners.

TO MAKE THE CUPCAKES

1. In a small bowl, whisk the flour, baking powder, and salt.

2. In a medium bowl, whisk the brown sugar, peanut butter, and butter until smooth.

3. One at a time, add the egg white, vanilla, and milk, whisking well after each addition until combined.

4. Stir in the flour mixture just until combined. Fill the cupcake liners just under three-fourths full and press 4 or 5 chocolate chips into the center of each cupcake.

5. Bake for 16 to 19 minutes until a toothpick inserted near the center of a cupcake comes out clean (avoid hitting the molten chocolate in the center).

6. Cool the cupcakes in the tin for 10 minutes before transferring to a wire rack to cool completely, about 20 minutes.

TO MAKE THE BROWN SUGAR–PEANUT BUTTER FROSTING

In a medium bowl, whisk the peanut butter, powdered sugar, brown sugar, heavy cream, butter, and vanilla until smooth. Pipe onto the cupcakes and enjoy!

Ingredient Tip Natural peanut butters can be too oily for most baking. Choose a sweetened commercial brand for this recipe.

standard
muffin tin

PREP TIME
15 minutes

COOK TIME
16 to 20 minutes

COOLING OR
CHILLING TIME
25 to 30 minutes

SHELF LIFE
2 to 3 days

Pumpkin Cupcakes

MAKES 4 cupcakes

Did the Cream Cheese Pumpkin Bread (page 36) not have quite enough cream cheese for you? Try these cupcakes. Sweet and full of spice, they are moist, delicious, and topped with generous swirls of cream cheese frosting. Your cream cheese craving will be more than satisfied.

FOR THE CUPCAKES

½ cup all-purpose flour

½ teaspoon baking powder

¼ teaspoon ground cinnamon

⅛ teaspoon ground allspice

⅛ teaspoon ground nutmeg

⅛ teaspoon salt

¼ cup granulated sugar

¼ cup packed brown sugar

2 tablespoons vegetable oil

1 large egg white

¼ cup canned pumpkin purée

½ teaspoon vanilla extract

FOR THE CREAM CHEESE FROSTING

4 tablespoons unsalted butter,
    at room temperature

2 ounces cream cheese,
    at room temperature

¼ teaspoon vanilla extract

⅔ cup powdered sugar, sifted

Pinch salt

1. Preheat the oven to 350°F.

2. Line a muffin tin with four cupcake liners.

TO MAKE THE CUPCAKES

1. In a small bowl, whisk the flour, baking powder, cinnamon, allspice, nutmeg, and salt.

2. In a medium bowl, whisk the granulated sugar, brown sugar, and vegetable oil until well combined.

3. One at a time, add the egg white, pumpkin, and vanilla, whisking well after each addition until well combined.

4. Stir in the flour mixture just until combined. Fill the cupcake liners just two-thirds full. Do not overfill.

5. Bake for 16 to 20 minutes until a toothpick inserted into the center of a cupcake comes out clean.

6. Cool the cupcakes in the tin for 5 to 10 minutes before transferring to a cooling rack to cool completely before frosting, about 20 minutes.

TO MAKE THE CREAM CHEESE FROSTING

1. In a medium bowl, whisk the butter, cream cheese, and vanilla until smooth.

2. Add the powdered sugar and salt, and whisk until the sugar is completely incorporated. Transfer to a piping bag and pipe frosting onto the cooled cupcakes. Keep refrigerated in an airtight container.

Ingredient Tip Leftover pumpkin purée can be transferred to an airtight container and refrigerated for 5 to 7 days, or frozen for up to 3 months.

Banana Cupcakes with Caramelized Banana Whipped Cream Frosting

MAKES 4 cupcakes

standard
muffin tin

PREP TIME
20 minutes

COOK TIME
26 to 30 minutes

COOLING OR
CHILLING TIME
40 to 45 minutes

SHELF LIFE
2 to 3

If you're a fan of bananas, these might just be your new favorite cupcakes. The cake is lightly spiced and full of banana flavor, and the frosting is made by caramelizing banana slices in butter and brown sugar and whipping them into a light and fluffy whipped cream.

FOR THE CUPCAKES

½ cup all-purpose flour

¼ teaspoon baking soda

¼ teaspoon ground cinnamon

⅛ teaspoon salt

4 tablespoons unsalted butter, at room temperature

¼ cup granulated sugar

1 large egg

¼ cup mashed banana

2 tablespoons plain yogurt

½ teaspoon vanilla extract

FOR THE CARAMELIZED BANANA WHIPPED CREAM FROSTING

1 tablespoon unsalted butter, at room temperature

1 tablespoon packed brown sugar

½ ripe banana, cut in ½-inch slices

½ cup heavy (whipping) cream

2 teaspoons granulated sugar

1. Preheat the oven to 350°F.

2. Line a muffin tin with four cupcake liners.

TO MAKE THE CUPCAKES

1. In a small bowl, whisk the flour, baking soda, cinnamon, and salt.

2. In a medium bowl, cream together the butter and granulated sugar.

3. One at a time, add the egg, banana, yogurt, and vanilla, whisking well after each addition until combined.

4. Stir in the flour mixture just until combined. Fill the cupcake liners two-thirds full.

5. Bake for 16 to 20 minutes until a toothpick inserted into the center of a cupcake comes out clean.

6. Cool the cupcakes in the tin for 5 to 10 minutes before transferring to a rack to cool completely, about 20 minutes.

TO MAKE THE CARAMELIZED BANANA WHIPPED CREAM FROSTING

1. Place the mixer beaters or a whisk and a medium bowl in the freezer to chill.

2. In a small pan over medium-low heat, melt the butter.

3. Stir in the brown sugar just until the sugar is mixed in.

4. Add the banana slices in a single layer and cook for 3 to 5 minutes, stirring occasionally so the sugar doesn't burn and the bottoms of the bananas are lightly browned and look fried. Flip and cook for 2 to 3 minutes until the other side is cooked. With a slotted spoon, transfer the slices to a small bowl and use a potato masher or a fork to mash the bananas to a fine purée. Refrigerate for about 15 minutes until completely cool.

5. Once the bananas are cool, remove the whisk and bowl from the freezer and pour the heavy cream and granulated sugar into the bowl. With an electric mixer or whisk, beat the cream for 1 to 2 minutes (4 to 7 minutes if whipping by hand) until stiff peaks form.

6. Beat the cooled bananas in their bowl for a couple of seconds to fluff them up then use a rubber spatula to fold them into the whipped cream mixture, until they are well incorporated. Transfer the mixture to a piping bag and pipe over the cooled cupcakes. Refrigerate the cupcakes until serving.

Cooking Tip "Stiff peaks" means when you lift the whisk straight out of the cream, the peaks stand straight up and don't flop over. Stiff peaks are only required for piping cream. If you don't plan to pipe it, you only need medium peaks, when the cream holds its shape standing up, but the peaks flop over. This cream will be sturdy enough to spoon over the cupcakes.

Mini Bundt Pound Cakes

MAKES 2 to 3 mini Bundt cakes (see Tip)

2 or 3 mini
bundt cake pans

PREP TIME
20 minutes

COOK TIME
22 to 26 minutes

COOLING OR
CHILLING TIME
35 minutes

SHELF LIFE
2 to 3 days

Mini Bundt cakes are small-batch baking at peak adorable. These miniaturized cakes are sure to melt hearts with their cuteness, and, if their tiny stature doesn't do it, their fantastic taste and texture will. These are a simple buttery sweet with a fine crumb and slightly crisp exterior. When you top them with fresh fruit and whipped cream, they make a perfect teatime treat.

FOR THE CAKES

3 tablespoons unsalted butter,
   at room temperature, plus
   more for greasing the pans

½ cup sifted cake flour, plus more
   for flouring the pans

⅛ teaspoon salt

½ cup superfine sugar

1 large egg, at room temperature

½ teaspoon vanilla extract

3 tablespoons heavy
   (whipping) cream

FOR THE TOPPINGS

Powdered sugar

Whipped Cream, or Cream Cheese
   Whipped Cream (page 83)

1 cup fresh fruit

1. Preheat the oven to 350°F.

2. Grease and flour the mini Bundt pans.

TO MAKE THE CAKES

1. Into a medium bowl, sift together the cake flour and salt. Set aside.

2. In a medium bowl, with an electric mixer at high speed, cream together the butter and superfine sugar, scraping down the sides and bottom of the bowl as necessary.

3. Add the egg and vanilla. Beat for 1 minute. Scrape down the sides.

4. Turn the speed to low and add half the flour mixture, the heavy cream, and the remaining flour mixture, mixing well after each addition. Turn the speed to high and beat for 4 minutes, scraping the sides and the bottom of the bowl halfway through. The batter should be light and very smooth. Divide the batter between the prepared pans.

5. Bake for 22 to 26 minutes until the cakes are golden and a toothpick inserted into the cakes comes out clean.

6. Cool the cakes in the pans for at least 15 minutes before gently removing and transferring to a rack to cool completely for about 20 minutes.

7. Dust with powdered sugar or top with whipped cream and fresh fruit before serving.

Cooking Tip This recipe will make three mini Bundt cakes using ⅔-cup pans and two cakes using 1-cup pans. Cooking time will be on the lower end of the recommended range for the former and the higher for the latter. If you don't own mini Bundt pans, use a muffin tin to make pound cake cupcakes. This amount of batter will make about six cupcakes. Bake at the same temperature for 18 to 24 minutes.

Orange Cream Mini Bundt Cakes

MAKES 2 to 3 mini Bundt cakes

These mini Bundt cakes are an orange-flavored dream. Classic pound cake with an orange twist and crunchy orange cream glaze, they taste almost like an old-fashioned donut, without all the grease.

2 or 3 mini
Bundt cake pans

PREP TIME
20 minutes

COOK TIME
22 to 26 minutes

COOLING OR
CHILLING TIME
20 minutes

SHELF LIFE
2 to 3 days

FOR THE CAKES

3 tablespoons unsalted butter,
   at room temperature, plus
   more for greasing the pans

½ cup sifted cake flour, plus
   more for flouring the pans

⅛ teaspoon salt

½ cup superfine sugar

1 large egg, at room temperature

½ teaspoon vanilla extract

½ teaspoon grated orange zest

3 tablespoons heavy
   (whipping) cream

FOR THE ORANGE CREAM GLAZE

¼ cup powdered sugar, sifted

2 to 3 teaspoons heavy (whipping)
   cream, or milk, divided

¼ teaspoon grated orange zest

1. Preheat the oven to 350°F.

2. Grease and flour the mini Bundt pans.

TO MAKE THE CAKES

1. Into a small bowl, sift together the cake flour and salt. Set aside.

2. In a medium bowl, with an electric mixer on high, cream together the butter and superfine sugar until very light and fluffy. Scrape down the sides and bottom of the bowl and add the egg, vanilla, and orange zest. Beat for 1 minute.

3. Turn the speed to low and add half the flour mixture, all the heavy cream, and the remaining flour mixture, beating well after each addition.

4. Beat for 4 minutes at high speed until the mixture is smooth, scraping the sides and bottom of the bowl halfway through. Transfer the batter to the prepared pans.

5. Bake for 22 to 26 minutes until the tops are golden and a toothpick inserted into the center comes out clean.

6. Cool the cakes in the pans for 15 minutes before removing and adding the glaze.

TO MAKE THE ORANGE CREAM GLAZE

In a small bowl, whisk the powdered sugar, 2 teaspoons of heavy cream, and the orange zest until smooth. If the glaze is too thick, add more cream by the ¼ teaspoon until it reaches the desired consistency. Pour over the Bundt cakes and allow to set for 5 minutes before serving.

Variation Tip For a fun twist, replace the heavy cream in the glaze with the same amount of your favorite orange liqueur.

Strawberry Buttercream Layer Cake

MAKES 1 (2-layer, 6-inch) cake

6-inch cake pan
at least 2 inches tall

PREP TIME
30 minutes

COOK TIME
30 to 35 minutes

COOLING OR
CHILLING TIME
50 minutes

SHELF LIFE
3 to 4 days

This light and tender vanilla cake with strawberry buttercream and a jam center is a little stunner. Two tiny towering layers with light pink frosting flecked with puréed strawberries, it's definitely begging to be made for a special occasion.

It is made in a single pan and cut into layers, but don't worry, no crumbly difficult-to-handle cake here. Once completely cooled, the cake is easy to cut and work with. The thin layer of strawberry jam over the strawberry buttercream is optional, but delicious and highly recommended.

FOR THE CAKE

5 tablespoons unsalted butter, at
    room temperature, plus more for
    greasing the pan
1 cup cake flour, sifted, plus more for
    flouring the pan
½ teaspoon baking powder
¼ teaspoon baking soda
¼ teaspoon salt
⅔ cup granulated sugar
1 large egg
½ teaspoon vanilla extract
½ cup buttermilk

FOR THE STRAWBERRY FROSTING

¼ cup strawberry purée (4 or 5 large
    fresh strawberries pulsed in
    a blender or food processor
    until puréed)
1 teaspoon granulated sugar
8 tablespoons (1 stick) unsalted
    butter, at room temperature
2 cups powdered sugar,
    sifted, divided
1 tablespoon milk, or heavy
    (whipping) cream
¼ teaspoon vanilla extract

FOR THE FILLING (OPTIONAL)

3 tablespoons strawberry jam
Sprinkles (optional)

TO MAKE THE CAKE

1. Preheat the oven to 350°F.

2. Grease, flour, and line the cake pan with parchment paper.

3. In a small bowl, whisk the cake flour, baking powder, baking soda, and salt. Set aside.

4. In a large bowl, cream together the butter and granulated sugar until light and fluffy.

5. Beat in the egg and vanilla until well combined.

6. One at a time, stir in half the flour mixture, all the buttermilk, the remaining flour, and mix after each addition just until combined.

7. Transfer the batter to the prepared cake pan, filling it no more than three-fourths full, and gently smooth the top. Bake for 30 to 35 minutes, until the top is browned and a toothpick inserted into the center of the cake comes out mostly clean. Place the pan on a cooling rack to cool for at least 20 minutes.

8. After the cake has cooled in the pan, remove it. Put the cooling rack on top of the pan, put your hand on top of the rack, and turn it over so the cake pan is now on the top. Lift the cake pan off the cake and, if necessary, give the bottom a couple of taps. Gently peel off the parchment paper and let the cake finish cooling upside down. This will help flatten the top. Cool completely for about 30 minutes.

TO MAKE THE STRAWBERRY FROSTING

1. While the cake bakes, combine the strawberry purée and granulated sugar in a 1-quart saucepan over medium heat. Bring to a low simmer and cook, stirring often, for 2 to 3 minutes until reduced to 1 to 2 tablespoons. Remove from the heat. When completely cooled, cover with plastic wrap and refrigerate.

2. In a medium bowl, whisk the butter, 1 cup of powdered sugar, the milk, and vanilla until smooth.

CONTINUED

3. Beat in the strawberry purée until well combined.

4. Add the remaining 1 cup of powdered sugar and whisk until light and fluffy.

TO ASSEMBLE THE CAKE

1. Turn the cake right-side up. With a long serrated knife, carefully cut the cake horizontally into two layers. Transfer one layer to a serving plate or cake platter.

2. Spread slightly less than one-third of the frosting over the first layer.

3. Spread the strawberry jam (if using) over the frosting, before placing the top layer on the cake.

4. Spread the remaining two-thirds of the frosting over the rest of the cake. Start by placing all the frosting on top and spreading it outward across the top and down the sides.

5. Add sprinkles (if using) around the top edge of the cake for a cute and effortless look. Slice and serve.

Substitution Tip If you don't have fresh strawberries, make the buttercream with strawberry jam. Start with 1 tablespoon of jam when you would add the purée and add more to taste.

Death by Chocolate Sheet Cake

MAKES 1 (5-by-7-inch) cake

What we have here is a light and delicate chocolate cake, soft and gently sweet, smothered in a bold and glorious chocolate glaze. It's a fantastic contrast on the fork and so perfectly chocolatey for those times when you desperately need a chocolate fix. How many times can I say chocolate in one description? Chocolate.

5-by-7-inch
baking dish

PREP TIME
15 minutes

COOK TIME
14 to 16 minutes

COOLING OR
CHILLING TIME
10 to 15 minutes

SHELF LIFE
3 to 4 days

FOR THE CAKE

4 tablespoons unsalted butter, at room temperature, plus more for greasing the dish

¼ cup all-purpose flour

1 tablespoon unsweetened natural cocoa powder

½ teaspoon baking powder

¼ teaspoon salt

¼ cup granulated sugar

1 large egg white

¼ teaspoon vanilla extract

2 tablespoons milk

2 tablespoons hot coffee, or water

FOR THE CHOCOLATE GLAZE

2 tablespoons unsalted butter

1 tablespoon milk

1 teaspoon light corn syrup

½ teaspoon vanilla extract

2 heaping tablespoons chopped semisweet chocolate

½ cup powdered sugar, sifted

1. Preheat the oven to 350°F.

2. Grease the baking dish.

TO MAKE THE CAKE

1. In a small bowl, whisk the flour, cocoa powder, baking powder, and salt.

2. In a medium bowl, cream together the butter and granulated sugar.

3. Whisk in the egg white and vanilla until well combined.

4. One at a time, stir in half the flour mixture, all the milk, the remaining flour mixture, and mix after each addition just until combined.

CONTINUED

5. Stir in the coffee and pour the batter into the prepared dish. Bake for 14 to 16 minutes, or until a toothpick inserted into the center of the cake comes out mostly clean.

6. Cool for at least 5 minutes before starting the glaze.

TO MAKE THE CHOCOLATE GLAZE

1. In a 1-quart saucepan over medium heat, combine the butter, milk, corn syrup, and vanilla. Heat, whisking until the butter melts and the ingredients are mixed.

2. Add the chocolate and whisk until it is melted and incorporated.

3. Reduce the heat to low and add the powdered sugar. Whisk until the sugar is melted. Remove from the heat and pour over the slightly cooled cake.

4. Let the glaze set for 5 to 10 minutes and serve the cake directly from the dish. Slice and enjoy with a strong cup of coffee.

Cooking Tip Wait until the cake is done baking before starting the glaze. While it doesn't completely harden, the glaze does set as it cools and will not pour if it sits for longer than a couple of minutes.

Mom's Carrot Cake

MAKES 1 (5-by-7-inch) cake

This carrot cake is another recipe from the Yabiku family archives. The original fills a 9-by-13-inch casserole dish and is my mom's go-to potluck dessert. When I was a kid, she'd always make it the night before a party, and if we were lucky, my sisters and I would get to lick the frosting bowl before it was time to brush our teeth. When she'd come home from the event the next day, we'd run to the door to see if there were any leftovers. There almost never were. This version is a miniature version of her perfect—and perfectly delicious—cake. It's baked in a 5-by-7-inch dish, making it just the right size to feed you and your closest work confidants, or three hungry adolescent girls.

5-by-7-inch
baking dish

PREP TIME
15 minutes

COOK TIME
24 to 27 minutes

COOLING OR
CHILLING TIME
1 hour, 15 minutes

SHELF LIFE
3 to 4 days

FOR THE CAKE

Butter or shortening, for
    greasing the baking dish

½ cup all-purpose flour

1 teaspoon baking soda

½ teaspoon ground cinnamon

½ teaspoon ground allspice

¼ teaspoon salt

½ cup granulated sugar

¼ cup vegetable oil

1 large egg

⅔ cup grated carrots

FOR THE FROSTING

4 tablespoons unsalted butter,
    at room temperature

2 ounces cream cheese,
    at room temperature

¼ teaspoon vanilla extract

⅔ cup powdered sugar, sifted

Pinch salt

1. Preheat the oven to 350°F.

2. Grease the baking dish.

TO MAKE THE CAKE

1. In a small bowl, whisk the flour, baking soda, cinnamon, allspice, and salt.

2. In a medium bowl, whisk the granulated sugar, vegetable oil, and egg until well combined. Stir in the flour mixture and with a rubber spatula, fold in the carrots. Transfer the batter to the prepared dish.

CONTINUED

3. Bake for 24 to 27 minutes until a toothpick inserted into the center of the cake comes out clean.

4. Remove from the oven, place on a cooling rack, and cool completely, about 45 minutes, before frosting.

TO MAKE THE FROSTING

1. In a small bowl, whisk the butter, cream cheese, and vanilla until smooth.

2. Add the powdered sugar and salt and whisk until well combined and fluffy.

3. Spread the frosting over the cake. Chill for 30 minutes in the refrigerator. Serve the cake directly from the dish. Cover and refrigerate any leftovers.

Cooking Tip To get perfectly smooth and silky cream cheese frosting, you need to do three things: 1. Make sure the cream cheese is completely at room temperature before you begin so it will mix in easily. 2. Whisk the butter and cream cheese (and vanilla) before adding the dry ingredients so if there are any lumps, you can beat them out before the sugar makes that almost impossible. 3. Sift the powdered sugar before whisking it so you don't have sugar lumps in the frosting. If you don't mind a few lumps, you can skip sifting the sugar (and the extra dish to wash). It's purely for aesthetics.

Chocolate Red Wine Cake with Cream Cheese Whipped Cream

MAKES 1 (6-inch) cake

I like saying the name of this dessert because it sounds fancy and complicated, but it's actually quite simple and very easy. The cake is a short, slightly humble chocolate construction with just a hint of red wine in the batter. The red wine, chocolate ganache, and rich cream cheese whipped cream turn it into something special. It would be a perfect way to end a great date night (or, let's face it, a really bad one).

6-inch
cake pan

PREP TIME
25 minutes

COOK TIME
20 to 24 minutes

COOLING OR
CHILLING TIME
55 minutes

SHELF LIFE
2 to 3 days

FOR THE CAKE

Butter or shortening, for
   greasing the pan
2 tablespoons unsweetened
   natural cocoa powder, plus
   more for coating the pan
½ cup all-purpose flour
½ teaspoon baking powder
¼ teaspoon salt
¼ cup vegetable oil
¼ cup granulated sugar
1 large egg
2 tablespoons dry red wine
2 tablespoons sour cream
¼ teaspoon vanilla extract

FOR THE RED WINE CHOCOLATE GANACHE

½ cup chopped semisweet chocolate
2 teaspoons vegetable oil
2 teaspoons heavy (whipping) cream
2 teaspoons dry red wine

FOR THE CREAM CHEESE WHIPPED CREAM

¼ cup heavy (whipping) cream
1 ounce cream cheese, at room
   temperature
2 tablespoons granulated sugar
¼ teaspoon vanilla extract
Pinch salt

1. Preheat the oven to 350°F.

2. Grease and dust the cake pan with cocoa powder, and line it with parchment paper.

CONTINUED

TO MAKE THE CAKE

1. In a small bowl, whisk the flour, cocoa powder, baking powder, and salt.

2. In a medium bowl, whisk the oil, sugar, and egg. Whisk in the red wine, sour cream, and vanilla until smooth.

3. Stir in the flour mixture just until combined and transfer the batter to the prepared cake pan.

4. Bake for 16 to 20 minutes until a toothpick inserted into the center of the cake comes out mostly clean.

5. Cool the cake in the pan for 20 minutes on a cooling rack before removing it from the pan to cool completely for 30 minutes.

TO MAKE THE RED WINE CHOCOLATE GANACHE

1. In a 1-quart saucepan over medium-low heat, combine the chocolate, oil, heavy cream, and red wine. Whisk until melted and smooth. Remove from the heat and cool for 5 minutes until the mixture is quite thick, but still pourable.

2. Place the cooled cake on a serving plate and pour the ganache over the top. Use a knife to spread the ganache gently so it coats the top of the cake and drips over the edge in places.

TO MAKE THE CREAM CHEESE WHIPPED CREAM

1. Place a medium bowl and a whisk or the mixer beaters in the freezer for 15 minutes. Once chilled, remove them from the freezer and pour the heavy cream into the bowl. Beat until stiff peaks form.

2. In a second medium bowl, whisk the cream cheese, sugar, and vanilla until smooth. With a rubber spatula, fold in the whipped cream.

3. Spoon the cream cheese whipped cream over slices of cake and serve. The cake can be stored, covered, at room temperature. The whipped cream should be refrigerated in an airtight container.

Ingredient Tip The red wine taste in this cake is mild and not at all over-powering, but it is the base upon which the rest of the flavors are built. Use a good wine that you enjoy!

CHAPTER FOUR

Cookies & Bars

The wide array of cookies and bars in this chapter starts with some simple classics like Chocolate Chip Cookies (page 92) and Fudgy Chocolate Brownies (page 101), but before long, you'll be whipping up delights such as Snickerdoodle Sandwiches with Eggnog Buttercream (page 99) and Leftover Halloween Candy Blondies (page 108). As these are small-batch recipes, you can cook right through this chapter and have a taste of every one.

Tips & Techniques

Cookies are usually simple affairs, but there are some baking missteps—such as failing to refrigerate cookie dough when the recipe calls for it or using the wrong cocoa powder—that can result in a sub-par batch. Check out these tips to solve those problems.

Lining Baking Sheets You *can* bake cookies on a greased baking sheet, but parchment paper and silicone baking mats are a baker's best friends. They ensure cookies never stick, and help protect the cookie bottoms so you get even baking without burned bottoms.

Refrigerating Dough I know. No one wants to wait two hours before baking their cookies—but it's an important step that can't be skipped when the recipe calls for it. Some doughs need to chill so the ingredients firm up and hold their shape in the oven. If you bake dough before it's ready, you'll get puddles instead of cookies.

A Note on Cocoa Powder All recipes in this chapter use unsweetened natural cocoa powder only. Dutch-processed cocoa powder can't be used because these recipes need the acidity in natural cocoa powder to activate their leavening (Dutch-process is alkaline and can't do it). Dutch-processed cocoa can be a substitute for natural cocoa in some desserts, but not in the recipes in this chapter. Kitchen chemistry!

What to Do with Extra Whites Many recipes use only an egg yolk. You could throw away that egg white, or freeze it in an ice cube tray, store it in a freezer bag, and thaw it when needed. In case you're wondering, extra yolks can be refrigerated in an airtight container for about 24 hours. They don't freeze well.

Testing for Doneness

We'll rely on visual clues for the cookies, and the old toothpick trick for most bars, brownies, and blondies. Cookies have more wiggle room than muffins and cupcakes regarding doneness because underdone versus overdone is a matter of opinion. So if you have strong feelings on the subject, trust your instincts.

Storing

Bars, brownies, blondies, and cookies are simple to store. Unless they contain perishable ingredients, they do best on the counter in an airtight container and will, generally, be at their freshest if eaten within 4 or 5 days. Uncooked dough will keep in the refrigerator (wrapped) for up to 24 hours.

Too Many Sweets

These recipes (mostly) make 6 cookies and 2 (large) bars, brownies, or blondies, but sometimes even a small-batch recipe is too much. For the recipes in this chapter, that's not a problem! Cookies and brownies freeze quite well for eating later. Cookies can be frozen baked or raw. To freeze dough, prepare the cookies up to the point when you would put them into the oven, and stick them on a plate and freeze them instead. Once the cookies are frozen solid, you can store them in a freezer bag without them sticking together. When ready to bake, do so at the recommended temperature for just a couple minutes longer than the recipe calls for.

To freeze baked cookies and brownies, freeze them in an airtight container until you are ready to eat them. Thaw on a cooling rack or enjoy a frozen treat on a warm day. Frozen dough and baked goods are best if used and eaten within 2 to 3 months.

Caroline's (Shortbread) Cookies

silicone
baking mat

PREP TIME
10 minutes

COOK TIME
9 to 12 minutes

COOLING OR
CHILLING TIME
1 hour, 10 minutes

SHELF LIFE
4 to 5 days

MAKES 6 small cookies

Shortbread is one of the world's most delicious and versatile cookie doughs. You can scoop it, slice it, cut it into shapes—if you can imagine it, shortbread can probably do it. Not bad for a cookie made with just three ingredients, plus a pinch of salt. My sister Caroline introduced me to the delicious simplicity of the homemade shortbread cookie, so we're making them her favorite way: bite-size and rolled in as much crunchy sugar as possible.

4 tablespoons unsalted butter, at
   room temperature

2 tablespoons powdered sugar

½ cup all-purpose flour

Pinch salt

2 tablespoons coarse (sanding) sugar

1. In a medium bowl, cream together the butter and powdered sugar for about 1 minute until light and fluffy.

2. Stir in the flour and salt, mixing until a thick dough forms. Turn out the dough onto a sheet of plastic wrap and wrap it tightly. Refrigerate for 1 hour.

3. Preheat the oven to 350°F.

4. Line a baking sheet with a silicone mat (or parchment paper). Place the coarse sugar into a small bowl.

5. Divide the dough into six equal balls and roll each in the coarse sugar. Place the cookies on the prepared sheet and gently press each with a fork to about a ¾-inch thickness.

6. Bake for 9 to 12 minutes until the edges and bottoms of the cookies just start to brown.

7. Cool the cookies on the baking sheet for at least 10 minutes before eating.

Variation Tip For a fancier cookie, roll out the dough on a lightly floured surface and cut it into any shape you like. Bake for 6 to 10 minutes, depending on the size of the cookie. You'll know they're done as soon as the edges start to turn golden.

Savory Cheddar Cookies

MAKES about 16 bite-size cookies

Picture a rainy day, a bowl of soup, and a couple of cheesy, savory short-bread cookies. Can you imagine anything better? These cookies are made with equal parts (by weight) cheese, flour, and butter, and are like a grown-up version of your favorite cheesy store-bought cracker. But be warned, once you try this homemade version, the ones that come out of a box will pale in comparison.

4 tablespoons unsalted butter, at room temperature

½ cup all-purpose flour, plus more for flouring the work surface and the rolling pin

½ cup shredded sharp Cheddar cheese

Pinch salt

silicone baking mat

PREP TIME
10 minutes

COOK TIME
8 to 11 minutes

COOLING OR CHILLING TIME
1 hour, 15 minutes

SHELF LIFE
4 to 5 days

1. In a medium bowl, cream the butter.

2. Stir in the flour and Cheddar cheese until a thick dough forms. Turn out the dough onto a sheet of plastic wrap and wrap it tightly. Refrigerate for at least 1 hour.

3. Preheat the oven to 350°F.

4. Line a baking sheet with a silicone mat (or parchment paper).

5. On a well-floured surface and with a floured rolling pin, roll out the dough to a ¼-inch thickness. With a shot glass or cookie cutter, cut out 1½-inch rounds, gathering up and rerolling any scraps as necessary. Transfer the cookies to the prepared sheet and sprinkle lightly with salt. If the dough becomes soft and sticky, refrigerate it for 10 to 15 minutes before baking so it firms back up.

6. Bake for 8 to 11 minutes until lightly browned.

7. Cool the cookies on the sheet for 15 minutes before eating.

Cooking Tip If you don't have a shot glass or a cookie cutter handy, use a pizza cutter to cut the dough into 1-by-1-inch squares. Squeeze the dough scraps back together and reroll until you have used all the dough.

Chocolate Chip Cookies

silicone
baking mat

PREP TIME
10 minutes

COOK TIME
10 to 12 minutes

COOLING OR
CHILLING TIME
1 hour, 40 minutes

SHELF LIFE
4 to 5 days

MAKES 6 cookies

These are perfect chocolate chip cookies. They are big, but not ridiculously so, packed with just the right amount of chocolate, and are the ideal texture. A little crisp at the edges, soft and chewy in the centers. And since we use just an egg yolk in the batter, they brown beautifully. These are Instagram-worthy cookies that everyone will be drooling over.

½ cup plus 1 tablespoon
   all-purpose flour
¼ teaspoon baking soda
⅛ teaspoon baking powder
⅛ teaspoon salt
4 tablespoons unsalted butter,
   at room temperature

¼ cup packed brown sugar
2 tablespoons granulated sugar
1 large egg yolk
½ teaspoon vanilla extract
½ cup semisweet chocolate chips

1. In a small bowl, whisk the flour, baking soda, baking powder, and salt.

2. In a medium bowl, cream together the butter, brown sugar, and granulated sugar for about 1 minute until light and fluffy.

3. One at a time, add the egg yolk and vanilla, whisking well after each addition until combined.

4. Stir in the flour mixture just until combined. Fold in the chocolate chips. Cover the bowl with plastic wrap and refrigerate for at least 90 minutes, or up to 24 hours.

5. Preheat the oven to 375°F.

6. Line a baking sheet with a silicone mat (or parchment paper).

7. Divide the dough into 6 equal balls, each about the size of a golf ball, and place them on the prepared sheet at least 2 inches apart.

8. Bake for 10 to 12 minutes until the edges are browned and the centers lose most of their shiny, undercooked look.

9. Cool the cookies on the baking sheet for at least 10 minutes before eating.

Cooking Tip For the prettiest, most photogenic cookies, reserve a few chocolate chips and gently press 2 to 4 into the tops of the cookies before baking so you are guaranteed to have plenty of chocolate showing in your finished product.

Double Chocolate Chip Cookies

silicone
baking mat

PREP TIME
15 minutes

COOK TIME
10 to 12 minutes

COOLING OR
CHILLING TIME
2 hours, 10 minutes

SHELF LIFE
4 to 5 days

MAKES 6 large cookies

Fellow chocolate lovers, this is a cookie recipe just for us. Rich and fudgy doesn't even begin to describe the base of this cookie, and with a brimming half cup of chocolate chips packed inside, there is enough good stuff to satisfy even the most hard-core chocoholic.

½ cup plus 2 tablespoons
    all-purpose flour

⅓ cup unsweetened natural
    cocoa powder

¼ teaspoon baking soda

⅛ teaspoon salt

5 tablespoons unsalted butter,
    at room temperature

3 tablespoons packed brown sugar

3 tablespoons granulated sugar

1 large egg white

½ teaspoon vanilla extract

½ cup semisweet chocolate chips

1. In a small bowl, whisk the flour, cocoa powder, baking soda, and salt.

2. In a medium bowl, cream together the butter, brown sugar, and granulated sugar for about 1 minute until light and fluffy.

3. One at a time, add the egg white and vanilla, whisking well after each addition until combined.

4. Stir in the flour mixture just until combined and fold in the chocolate chips. Cover tightly with plastic wrap and refrigerate for at least 2 hours, or up to 24.

5. Preheat the oven to 350°F.

6. Line a baking sheet with a silicone mat (or parchment paper).

7. Divide the dough into 6 equal balls and place them on the prepared sheet at least 2 inches apart. Flatten them slightly with the palm of your hand and bake for 10 to 12 minutes until the cookies look set.

8. Cool the cookies on the baking sheet for at least 10 minutes before devouring.

Variation Tip You can make these cookies triple, or even quadruple, chocolate chip cookies by mixing your chocolates. Try half white chocolate chips, half semisweet, or even a mixture of semisweet, white, and dark chocolate!

Hot Chocolate Cookies

silicone
baking mat

PREP TIME
15 minutes

COOK TIME
10 to 12 minutes

COOLING OR
CHILLING TIME
2 hours, 10 minutes

SHELF LIFE
4 to 5 days

MAKES 6 large cookies

My double chocolate chip cookies get a winter upgrade when we stuff them full of marshmallows and sprinkle them with crushed peppermints. These are for those chilly nights when you feel like a hot chocolate (cookie) with all the fixings.

2 hard peppermint candies

½ cup plus 2 tablespoons all-purpose flour

⅓ cup unsweetened natural cocoa powder

¼ teaspoon baking soda

⅛ teaspoon salt

5 tablespoons unsalted butter, at room temperature

3 tablespoons packed brown sugar

3 tablespoons granulated sugar

1 large egg white

½ teaspoon vanilla extract

⅓ cup semisweet chocolate chips

24 mini marshmallows

1. Place the peppermint candies in a plastic bag or between two sheets of plastic wrap and give them a couple light thumps with a rolling pin or the bottom of a glass until they are broken into pieces. Set aside.

2. In a small bowl, whisk the flour, cocoa powder, baking soda, and salt.

3. In a medium bowl, cream together the butter, brown sugar, and granulated sugar for about 1 minute until light and fluffy.

4. Add the egg white and beat for about 1 minute until well combined.

5. Whisk in the vanilla. Stir in the flour mixture just until combined and fold in the chocolate chips. Cover the bowl in plastic wrap and refrigerate for at least 2 hours, or up to 24.

6. Preheat the oven to 350°F.

7. Line a baking sheet with a silicone mat (or parchment paper).

8. Divide the dough into 6 equal balls. Squish the first ball into a disk between the palms of your hands and place 4 mini marshmallows in the center. Fold the edges of the dough up so the marshmallows are completely covered and reform the dough into a ball. If any seams remain, make sure to place the cookies on the baking sheet seam-side up. Repeat with the remaining dough and marshmallows.

9. Top each cookie with some peppermint candy shards and press firmly on each with the palm of your hand so they are slightly flattened on the sheet.

10. Bake for 10 to 12 minutes until the edges look set and the centers are no longer shiny.

11. Cool the cookies on the baking sheet for 10 minutes before serving.

Cooking Tip If you don't have mini marshmallows on hand, cut 3 regular marshmallows in half to use instead.

Variation Tip To make Mexican hot chocolate cookies, add a pinch each of cinnamon and cayenne pepper or chili powder to the dough.

Peanut Butter Cookies

silicone
baking mat

PREP TIME
10 minutes

COOK TIME
8 to 11 minutes

COOLING OR
CHILLING TIME
10 minutes

SHELF LIFE
4 to 5 days

MAKES 6 cookies

In my book, a good peanut butter cookie should be soft and rich, but not so soft that it falls apart in your hands and not so rich that you may as well just eat a spoonful of peanut butter. A good peanut butter cookie is sweet, but not too sweet and neither crunchy nor chewy, but somehow a little bit of both. A good peanut butter cookie is a joy and a rarity. This is a good peanut butter cookie.

½ cup all-purpose flour

¼ teaspoon baking soda

¼ teaspoon salt

⅓ cup peanut butter (creamy or chunky)

3 tablespoons unsalted butter, at room temperature

3 tablespoons packed brown sugar

2 tablespoons granulated sugar

1 large egg yolk

½ teaspoon vanilla extract

1. Preheat the oven to 350°F.

2. Line a baking sheet with a silicone mat (or parchment paper).

3. In a small bowl, whisk the flour, baking soda, and salt.

4. In a medium bowl, whisk the peanut butter, butter, brown sugar, granulated sugar, egg yolk, and vanilla until smooth.

5. Stir in the flour mixture just until combined. Scoop the dough and roll it into 6 balls. Place them on the prepared sheet and use a fork to press the dough firmly in a crosshatch pattern.

6. Bake for 8 to 11 minutes until the edges look set but the cookies are still pale.

7. Cool the cookies on the baking sheet for at least 10 minutes before eating or moving, as the cookies will be very soft until they cool.

Cooking Tip If you like a crispier peanut butter cookie, bake for 10 to 12 minutes until the edges of the cookies begin to darken.

Snickerdoodle Sandwiches with Eggnog Buttercream

MAKES 6 cookie sandwiches

Merry Christmas! What's that you say? It's not Christmas? Well, it is if you are eating one of these. I'll admit, Snickerdoodle Sandwiches with Eggnog Buttercream sounds a bit like a mad lib of random food stuffs, but they make perfect sense the minute you bite into one and the eggnog buttercream joins the cinnamon snickerdoodles in a chorus of "Deck the Halls" all the way across your tongue.

2 silicone
baking mats

PREP TIME
20 minutes

COOK TIME
16 to 20 minutes

COOLING OR
CHILLING TIME
30 minutes

SHELF LIFE
3 to 4 days

FOR THE CINNAMON SUGAR

1 tablespoon granulated sugar

1 teaspoon ground cinnamon

FOR THE COOKIES

¾ cup all-purpose flour

½ teaspoon cream of tartar

¼ teaspoon baking soda

Pinch salt

2 tablespoons unsalted butter,
   at room temperature

2 tablespoons shortening

¼ cup plus 2 tablespoons
   granulated sugar

1 large egg

½ teaspoon vanilla extract

FOR THE EGGNOG BUTTERCREAM

4 tablespoons unsalted butter,
   at room temperature

¾ cup powdered sugar, sifted

⅛ teaspoon ground nutmeg

1 teaspoon to 1 tablespoon eggnog

1. Preheat the oven to 400°F.

2. Line 2 baking sheets with silicone mats (or parchment paper).

TO MAKE THE CINNAMON SUGAR

In a small bowl, mix the granulated sugar and cinnamon and set aside.

CONTINUED

TO MAKE THE COOKIES

1. In a small bowl, whisk the flour, cream of tartar, baking soda, and salt.

2. In a medium bowl, cream together the butter, shortening, and granulated sugar for about 1 minute until light and fluffy.

3. Crack the egg into a small bowl and whisk well. Transfer 1½ tablespoons of whisked egg to the creamed butter and sugar. Discard the remaining egg. Add the vanilla and whisk until well combined.

4. Stir in the flour mixture until smooth.

5. Roll the dough into 12 balls each about half the size of a golf ball. Roll each in the cinnamon sugar until completely coated. Divide the cookies between the prepared sheets.

6. Bake the sheets one at a time for 8 to 10 minutes each until the bottom edges of the cookies are just barely browned. Do not overcook!

7. Cool the cookies on the sheets for 10 minutes before transferring to a cooling rack to cool completely, about 20 minutes.

TO MAKE THE EGGNOG BUTTERCREAM

1. Once the cookies are cool, in a medium bowl, whisk the butter, powdered sugar, nutmeg, and enough eggnog to get a smooth consistency. Transfer the buttercream to a disposable plastic bag (piping the frosting makes for neater cookie sandwiches), and snip off a small corner of the bag.

2. Pair the cookies by size. Take 1 cookie from each pair and, starting in the center, pipe frosting spiraling outward until about ¼ inch from the edge. Place the mate on top and press gently until the frosting fills out to the edge of the sandwich.

Substitution Tip If you want to omit the eggnog flavor, use heavy (whipping) cream or milk instead, omit the nutmeg, and add ¼ teaspoon vanilla and ¼ teaspoon ground cinnamon.

Fudgy Chocolate Brownies

MAKES 2 bars

These are the best and easiest brownies in town. Fudgy and rich, all you need is one bowl, a whisk, and a baking pan. That's it. A no-fuss, no-effort treat this good and easy is a dangerous and handy recipe to have in your baking arsenal.

4 tablespoons unsalted butter, melted and slightly cooled, plus more for greasing the pan

½ cup granulated sugar

1 large egg

½ teaspoon vanilla extract

¼ cup all-purpose flour

3 tablespoons unsweetened natural cocoa powder, sifted

⅛ teaspoon baking powder

⅛ teaspoon salt

9-by-5-inch
loaf pan

PREP TIME
5 minutes

COOK TIME
22 to 25 minutes

COOLING OR
CHILLING TIME
15 to 20 minutes

SHELF LIFE
3 to 4 days

1. Preheat the oven to 350°F.

2. Grease the loaf pan and line it with parchment paper.

3. In a medium bowl, whisk the melted butter and sugar until well combined.

4. Add the egg and vanilla and whisk well.

5. Add the flour, cocoa powder (you run the risk of lumps if it is not sifted), baking powder, and salt. Stir together just until combined. Transfer the batter to the prepared pan. Spread it out so it covers most of the bottom.

6. Bake for 22 to 25 minutes until a toothpick inserted into the center comes out mostly clean.

7. Cool the brownies in the pan for 15 to 20 minutes before slicing and serving.

Variation Tip To make a brownie sundae, serve brownies warm with a scoop of ice cream, topped with Fudge Sauce (page 105, from the Chocolate Chip Cookie Blondie Skillet Sundae), and Whipped Cream (page 130).

S'mores Brownies

MAKES 2 bars

9-by-5-inch
loaf pan

PREP TIME
15 minutes

COOK TIME
28 to 31 minutes

COOLING OR
CHILLING TIME
15 minutes

SHELF LIFE
3 to 4 days

These s'mores brownies bake on a graham cracker crust, are studded with chunks of your favorite s'mores chocolate bar, and topped with toasted marshmallows. They are everything great about camping and s'mores without the actual camping.

Cooking spray, for preparing
   the loaf pan
¼ cup graham cracker crumbs
   (2½ graham crackers)
¼ cup all-purpose flour
3 tablespoons unsalted butter,
   melted and slightly cooled

2 tablespoons packed brown sugar
1 recipe Fudgy Chocolate Brownies
   batter (page 101)
1 (1.5-ounce) chocolate bar,
   roughly chopped
1 cup mini marshmallows

1. Preheat the oven to 350°F.

2. Line a loaf pan with aluminum foil (we use foil here because parchment paper should not be used under the broiler). Spray the foil with cooking spray.

3. In a small bowl, stir together the graham cracker crumbs, flour, melted butter, and brown sugar until thick.

4. Press the crumb mixture into the prepared pan, spreading it and pressing down firmly to cover the bottom. Bake for 5 minutes until the crust is just slightly darkened and looks set.

5. Top with the brownie batter, gently spreading it to cover the crust completely. Sprinkle the chopped chocolate over the top.

6. Bake for 22 to 24 minutes until a toothpick inserted in the center comes out mostly clean.

7. Top with the mini marshmallows and turn the broiler to high. Broil for 1 to 2 minutes, just until the marshmallows are toasted and slightly puffed up.

8. Cool the brownies in the pan for at least 15 minutes before removing from the pan and slicing.

Cooking Tip Don't walk away from marshmallows under the broiler. They cook very quickly and can go from pale to burning in a matter of seconds. As soon as they begin to puff up and brown on top, remove the pan. If they puff up too much, they will completely deflate when you take them out of the oven, leaving you with a sticky mess on the top of your brownies.

Chocolate Cream Cheese Swirl Brownies

9-by-5-inch
loaf pan

PREP TIME
15 minutes

COOK TIME
22 to 25 minutes

COOLING OR
CHILLING TIME
15 minutes

SHELF LIFE
3 to 4 days

MAKES 2 bars

Do you know what happens to Oreos when they are baked into brownies? They become just slightly softened and crumbly and almost melt in your mouth. Do you know what happens when you add a swirl of sweet cream cheese over that? Magic, my friend. Magic is what happens.

1 tablespoon unsalted butter, at room temperature, plus more for greasing the pan

8 Oreo cookies

3 ounces cream cheese, at room temperature

1 teaspoon vanilla extract

½ cup powdered sugar

1 recipe Fudgy Chocolate Brownies batter (page 101)

1. Preheat the oven to 350°F.

2. Grease the loaf pan and line it with parchment paper.

3. Line the bottom of the prepared pan with the Oreos.

4. In a small bowl, whisk the butter, cream cheese, vanilla, and powdered sugar until fully incorporated and smooth. Using a rubber spatula, swirl this mixture into the prepared brownie batter, stirring only enough to distribute it throughout the batter. Do not overmix or your ribbons of cream cheese will disappear. Spread the batter over the Oreos, making sure the batter covers most of the bottom.

5. Bake for 22 to 25 minutes until a toothpick inserted into the center comes out mostly clean.

6. Cool the brownies in the pan for at least 15 minutes before lifting them out of the pan and slicing them.

7. Refrigerate leftovers (you have leftovers?) in an airtight container.

Variation Tip These brownies can be made with almost any type of store-bought hard cookie. Experiment with different varieties to find the combination you like best. I think a peanut butter cookie base would be divine!

Chocolate Chip Cookie Blondie Skillet Sundae

MAKES 1 (6-inch) dessert

Is it a cookie? Is it a blondie? It's neither. It's both. It's delicious so who cares? A giant light and fluffy chocolate chip cookie (or very small and pretty dense chocolate chip blondie) baked in a cast iron skillet and topped with a scoop of ice cream and homemade fudge sauce. It's a perfectly indulgent dessert that requires two spoons, one for you and your best other—or one for each hand.

FOR THE CHOCOLATE CHIP BLONDIE

2 tablespoons unsalted butter, melted and slightly cooled

1 large egg yolk

¼ cup packed brown sugar

¼ teaspoon vanilla extract

¼ cup all-purpose flour

⅛ teaspoon baking powder

Pinch salt

⅓ cup semisweet chocolate chips

FOR THE FUDGE SAUCE

1 tablespoon unsalted butter

1½ tablespoons heavy (whipping) cream, divided

1 tablespoon granulated sugar

¼ teaspoon vanilla extract

3 tablespoons chopped semisweet chocolate

Pinch salt

1 large scoop ice cream of choice, for serving

Preheat the oven to 350°F.

TO MAKE THE CHOCOLATE CHIP BLONDIE

1. In a medium bowl, whisk the melted butter, egg yolk, brown sugar, and vanilla until well combined.

2. Stir in the flour, baking powder, and salt. Fold in the chocolate chips. Spread the batter into the skillet.

3. Bake for 17 to 21 minutes until the top loses its shiny, undercooked look.

4. Cool for at least 5 minutes until the skillet can be safely handled.

CONTINUED

6-inch ovenproof skillet

PREP TIME
10 minutes

COOK TIME
19 to 23 minutes

COOLING OR CHILLING TIME
5 minutes

SHELF LIFE
eat immediately

TO MAKE THE FUDGE SAUCE

1. In a 1-quart saucepan over medium heat, combine the butter, 1 tablespoon of heavy cream, the granulated sugar, and vanilla. Stir until the butter is melted and the mixture begins to simmer.

2. Reduce the heat to medium-low and add the chocolate and salt. Whisk until the chocolate is completely melted and the mixture is smooth.

3. Add the remaining ½ tablespoon of heavy cream, half a teaspoon at a time, until the sauce reaches the desired consistency. Remove from the heat.

TO SERVE

Put a large scoop of ice cream on top of the cookie blondie and pour warm fudge sauce over it.

Variation Tip If you prefer a caramel cookie blondie sundae, top with some quick Caramel Sauce (page 116). It takes only a minute or two longer to make than the fudge sauce and is so worth it!

Pumpkin Nutella Swirl Blondies

MAKES 2 bars

Looking for a pumpkin dessert but not quite ready to go full-on pumpkin pie yet? These blondies might be just the thing. Big on pumpkin flavor and, with a heavy drizzle of Nutella swirled into them, they make a dessert to be remembered.

4 tablespoons unsalted butter, at room temperature, plus more for greasing the pan

¼ cup packed brown sugar

2 tablespoons granulated sugar

¼ cup canned pumpkin purée

1 large egg yolk

½ teaspoon vanilla extract

½ cup all-purpose flour

¼ teaspoon baking soda

⅛ teaspoon salt

⅛ teaspoon ground cinnamon

⅛ teaspoon ground nutmeg

3 tablespoons Nutella

9-by-5-inch loaf pan

PREP TIME
15 minutes

COOK TIME
11 to 14 minutes

COOLING OR CHILLING TIME
20 minutes

SHELF LIFE
3 to 4 days

1. Preheat the oven to 350°F.

2. Grease a loaf pan and line it with parchment paper.

3. In a medium bowl, whisk the butter, brown sugar, and granulated sugar. Add the pumpkin, egg yolk, and vanilla and mix well.

4. Stir in the flour, baking soda, salt, cinnamon, and nutmeg until combined. Spread the batter in the prepared pan, making sure it covers the bottom.

5. In a small microwave-safe bowl, heat the Nutella in 30-second bursts on high, stirring after each, until it is pourable. In a wavy pattern, pour the Nutella over the batter. Swirl the mixture with a knife, then pull a clean knife lengthwise through the Nutella swirl twice for an attractive pattern.

6. Bake for 11 to 14 minutes until a toothpick inserted into the blondie comes out clean.

7. Cool the blondie in the pan for at least 20 minutes before removing and slicing.

Variation Tip If you are not a fan of Nutella, omit it and dust the blondies with cinnamon sugar and top with a dollop of whipped cream.

Leftover Halloween Candy Blondies

MAKES 2 bars

9-by-5-inch
loaf pan

PREP TIME
5 minutes

COOK TIME
20 to 23 minutes

COOLING OR
CHILLING TIME
15 minutes

SHELF LIFE
3 to 4 days

These bars are designed to hold up to a cup of your favorite candy. (I'm partial to M&Ms, but Snickers make a great and melty addition.) They are perfect when you need to find something to do with all that leftover candy you have lying around.

4 tablespoons unsalted butter, melted and slightly cooled, plus more for greasing the pan

¼ cup packed brown sugar

2 tablespoons granulated sugar

1 large egg

1 teaspoon vanilla extract

½ cup all-purpose flour

⅛ teaspoon baking powder

⅛ teaspoon salt

1 cup chopped candy of choice, divided

1. Preheat the oven to 350°F.

2. Grease a loaf pan and line it with parchment paper.

3. In a medium bowl, whisk the butter, brown sugar, granulated sugar, egg, and vanilla.

4. Add the flour, baking powder, and salt and stir to combine. Stir in roughly three-fourths of the candy. Pour the batter into the prepared pan and spread it over the bottom.

5. Scatter the remaining one-fourth of the candy over the batter.

6. Bake for 20 to 23 minutes until a toothpick inserted into the center comes out mostly clean. If there is no candy-free space, gently press the blondie with your finger. If it mostly springs back, it's done.

7. Cool the blondie in the pan for 15 minutes until it firms up enough to be removed from the pan without breaking. Slice and enjoy!

Cooking Tip If you use a candy with caramel in it, use a plastic dough scraper or plastic knife to unstick the blondie from the pan before removing it.

Shortbread Jam Bars

MAKES 2 bars

5-by-7-inch
baking dish

PREP TIME
20 minutes

COOK TIME
40 to 52 minutes

COOLING OR
CHILLING TIME
45 minutes

SHELF LIFE
3 to 4 days

Just buttery, crumbly shortbread with a fruity jam filling. So simple and yet one of the most sweetly satisfying treats around. It almost makes you feel bad for other desserts that try twice as hard without being half as good.

6 tablespoons unsalted butter, at room temperature, plus more for greasing the baking dish

¼ cup plus 2 tablespoons powdered sugar, sifted

2 tablespoons granulated sugar

2 teaspoons vanilla extract

¾ cup all-purpose flour

¼ teaspoon salt

⅓ cup jam of choice

1. Preheat the oven to 350°F.

2. Grease the baking dish and line it with parchment paper.

3. In a large bowl, whisk the butter, powdered sugar, and granulated sugar for at least 1 minute until light and fluffy. Whisk in the vanilla.

4. Stir in the flour and salt and mix until well combined and a sticky dough forms. Spread slightly more than one-third of the dough over the bottom of the prepared dish, pressing it to cover the bottom in an even layer. Wrap the remaining dough in plastic wrap and refrigerate.

5. Bake the base for 20 to 22 minutes until the edges just start to brown.

6. Cool for 15 minutes then spread the jam over the top.

7. Remove the remaining dough from the refrigerator and drop penny-size pieces of it over the jam until you have used all the shortbread and the top is mostly covered.

8. Bake for 20 to 30 minutes until lightly browned.

9. Cool for at least 30 minutes before removing from the dish and slicing.

Substitution Tip To make caramel bars instead of jam bars, use 3 ounces of caramel bits, melted according to the package instructions, in place of the jam.

Apple and Maple Blondies

MAKES 2 bars

5-by-7-inch
baking dish

PREP TIME
20 minutes

COOK TIME
20 to 24 minutes

COOLING OR
CHILLING TIME
20 to 25 minutes

SHELF LIFE
3 to 4 days

This is my favorite bar in this book. These blondies are a little cakier, a little fluffier, and a little lighter than the rest and are filled with cara-melized apples and topped with a buttery maple glaze. Once the pumpkin madness of October has passed every year, this is the fall dessert I find myself returning to over and over again.

FOR THE APPLE AND MAPLE BLONDIES

½ cup diced (¼-inch) Granny
    Smith apple
5 tablespoons unsalted butter, at
    room temperature, divided, plus
    more for greasing the baking dish
¼ cup packed brown sugar,
    plus 1 tablespoon
¾ teaspoon vanilla extract, divided
⅜ teaspoon ground
    cinnamon, divided
1 tablespoon granulated sugar

1 large egg yolk
½ cup all-purpose flour
¼ teaspoon baking powder
⅛ teaspoon salt

FOR THE MAPLE GLAZE

1 tablespoon unsalted butter, melted
¼ cup powdered sugar
½ teaspoon heavy (whipping) cream
⅛ teaspoon maple extract
⅛ teaspoon vanilla extract
⅛ teaspoon ground cinnamon

1. Preheat the oven to 350°F.

2. Grease the baking dish and line it with parchment paper.

TO MAKE THE APPLE AND MAPLE BLONDIES

1. In a 1- or 2-quart saucepan over medium heat, combine the apple, 1 tablespoon of butter, 1 tablespoon of brown sugar, ¼ teaspoon of vanilla, and ⅛ teaspoon of cinnamon. Heat, stirring occasionally, until the butter is melted and the mixture begins to sizzle. Cook for 2 to 3 minutes, just until the apple begins to soften. Remove from the heat and set aside.

2. In a medium bowl, whisk the remaining 4 tablespoons of butter, remaining ¼ cup of brown sugar, and the granulated sugar until well combined.

3. Add the egg yolk, the remaining ½ teaspoon of vanilla, and the remaining ¼ teaspoon of cinnamon. Mix well.

4. Whisk in the flour, baking powder, and salt just until combined. Transfer half of the batter to the prepared dish, gently spreading to cover the bottom.

5. Sprinkle the cooked apple over the top, making sure to include the caramelized sugar and butter mixture at the bottom of the saucepan.

6. Cover the apple with the remaining batter in dollops and spread it over the apple. Some apple will show through in spots.

7. Bake for 18 to 21 minutes, until browned and the center looks set.

8. Cool for at least 15 minutes before adding the glaze.

TO MAKE THE MAPLE GLAZE

In a small bowl, whisk the butter, powdered sugar, heavy cream, maple extract, vanilla, and cinnamon until smooth. Spread over the slightly cooled blondies. Let the glaze set for 5 to 10 minutes before eating.

Ingredient Tip If you don't have tart apples, most sweet varieties will work just fine (not Red Delicious—they become mushy when baked). Just add about ¼ teaspoon of freshly squeezed lemon juice to the diced apple before cooking to offset their sweetness.

CHAPTER FIVE

Cobblers, Crisps & Shortcakes

It's time to hit the farmers' market, because the recipes in this chapter—from savory cobblers packed full of fresh veggies to chocolate shortcakes loaded with ripe summer strawberries—are all about celebrating the simple joy of a perfect piece of produce.

Tips & Techniques

Fruity desserts, such as cobblers and crisps, are uniquely challenging. You can be less rigid about ingredients and techniques, because you are working with fresh produce, but you will never get exactly the same result twice. Here are a few tips to keep in mind as you navigate this (mostly) fruit-filled chapter.

How Much Sugar? Think of the sugar measurements in this chapter more like guidelines than rules. Since the sweetness of fresh fruit can vary, we have to be flexible when working with it. Taste the fruit before you start and use more or less sugar depending on how sweet it is.

Substitutions Fruit substitutions are encouraged! Use fresh fruit that is in season and that you like best. Similar fruits, such as different varieties of dark berries, can be swapped with minimal adjustment. Particularly sweet and juicy fruits, such as peaches, may need half the sugar and up to twice the amount of thickener as berries do, to keep the filling from becoming too sweet and runny.

Rubbing Butter into Flour For crisps, if you hate the feeling of butter under your fingers, you can use a pastry blender (or two knives) to cut the butter into the flour, but you get better results faster if you rub the butter and flour between your fingers until no large pieces remain and the mixture begins to form clumps. Start with very cold butter and, if it's a warm day, run your fingers under cold water for about 30 seconds before you begin.

Testing for Doneness

Testing cobblers and crisps for doneness is very easy. It's all about visual clues. The filling should be hot and bubbling and the top of the cobbler should be nicely browned.

Storing

All recipes in this chapter taste best fresh out of the oven. If possible, prepare them just before eating. If you have leftovers, cobblers and crisps can be covered and refrigerated, and shortcakes (without fruit or cream toppings) are fine in an airtight container on the counter.

Make It a Crumble

Crunchy crisp toppings not your thing? You can turn crisps into crumbles by omitting the crunchy ingredients in the topping, adding a little baking powder, and playing with the ingredient ratios a bit between the flour and butter (a little more, a little less . . .). For the crumble topping, you will need

⅓ cup all-purpose flour

2 tablespoons packed
   brown sugar

1 tablespoon
   granulated sugar

¼ teaspoon
   baking powder

¼ teaspoon ground cinnamon

⅛ teaspoon salt

3 tablespoons unsalted butter,
   just softened

In a small bowl, stir together the flour, brown sugar, granulated sugar, baking powder, cinnamon, and salt. Use your fingers or a fork to mix in the butter until rough crumbs form. Scatter this topping in crumbles over the fruit and bake as directed in the recipe until the fruit is bubbly and beautiful.

Caramel Apple Cobbler

MAKES 1 (5-by-7-inch) cobbler

5-by-7-inch
baking dish

PREP TIME
15 minutes

COOK TIME
41 to 48 minutes

COOLING OR
CHILLING TIME
5 minutes

SHELF LIFE
1 to 2 days

Grandma's classic apple cobbler just got even better with the addition of some quick homemade caramel. The apples are tart and sweet, the cobbler topping buttery and warm, and the caramel baked inside and drizzled over the top is a sugary delight.

FOR THE FILLING

1 cup peeled and thinly sliced
   Granny Smith apples

2 tablespoons packed brown sugar

1 tablespoon unsalted butter

½ teaspoon ground cinnamon

FOR THE CARAMEL SAUCE

¼ cup packed brown sugar

¼ cup heavy (whipping) cream

2 tablespoons unsalted butter

¼ teaspoon salt

½ teaspoon vanilla extract

FOR THE COBBLER BATTER

4 tablespoons unsalted butter, melted

½ cup all-purpose flour

½ cup granulated sugar

½ teaspoon baking powder

⅛ teaspoon salt

½ cup milk

½ teaspoon vanilla extract

Vanilla ice cream, for serving

Preheat the oven to 350°F.

TO MAKE THE FILLING

In a 2-quart saucepan over medium heat, combine the apples, brown sugar, butter, and cinnamon. Bring to a simmer and cook for 2 to 3 minutes just until the apples are softened. Remove from the heat and set aside.

TO MAKE THE CARAMEL SAUCE

1. In another small saucepan over medium heat, combine the brown sugar, heavy cream, butter, and salt. Heat until the butter melts. Mix well, bring to a low simmer, and cook for 4 to 5 minutes, stirring occasionally, until the mixture thickens into caramel. Remove from the heat and stir in the vanilla.

2. Add 2 tablespoons of caramel to the apples and stir to coat. Reserve the remaining caramel for serving with the cobbler.

TO MAKE THE COBBLER BATTER

1. Pour the melted butter into the baking dish.

2. In a medium bowl, whisk the flour, granulated sugar, baking powder, and salt.

3. Whisk in the milk slowly to avoid lumps, then whisk in the vanilla. Pour the batter into the baking dish over the butter. Do not stir.

4. Distribute the caramel apples evenly over the batter.

5. Place the dish into the oven with a baking sheet underneath to catch any drips. Bake for 35 to 40 minutes until the top is lightly browned and the fruit is bubbly.

6. Cool for at least 5 minutes before serving with a big scoop of vanilla ice cream and the remaining caramel sauce on the side.

Cooking Tip The caramel sauce can be made up to a week in advance. Simply refrigerate it in an airtight container and reheat it in the microwave to return it to a pourable consistency. This sauce is also great for drizzling over ice cream, brownies, or shortbread cookies.

Skillet Peach Cobbler

MAKES 1 (6-inch) cobbler

Desserts are immediately a hundred times cuter when served in a mini cast iron skillet, and this darling little peach cobbler is no exception. Served with a big scoop of vanilla ice cream, it's the perfect size for two to polish off after dinner. The hint of nutmeg accentuates the peachy flavor, and you'll be dreaming about the buttery cobbler topping for days.

6-inch cast iron skillet or other ovenproof mini skillet

PREP TIME
10 minutes

COOK TIME
25 to 35 minutes

COOLING OR CHILLING TIME
5 to 10 minutes

SHELF LIFE
1 to 2 days

2 tablespoons unsalted butter, melted

¼ cup granulated sugar, plus
  2 tablespoons, divided

¼ cup all-purpose flour

¼ teaspoon baking powder

Pinch salt

¼ cup milk

¼ teaspoon vanilla extract

½ cup peeled, sliced ripe peaches

⅛ teaspoon ground nutmeg

Ice cream of choice, for serving

1. Preheat the oven to 350°F.

2. Add the melted butter to the mini skillet.

3. In a small bowl, whisk ¼ cup of sugar, the flour, baking powder, and salt. Slowly whisk in the milk and vanilla, mixing well. Pour the batter over the melted butter in the skillet.

4. Using the same bowl, toss the peaches with the remaining 2 tablespoons of sugar and the nutmeg. Put the peach slices into the skillet, spreading them over the batter as evenly as possible.

5. Bake for 25 to 35 minutes until the cobbler top is nicely browned and looks set.

6. Cool for 5 to 10 minutes until the skillet is safe to handle. Top with a scoop of ice cream and serve in the skillet.

Cooking Tip If you don't own a 6-inch skillet, you can double the recipe and bake it in a 5-by-7-inch baking dish. Cooking time will increase by 10 minutes, to 35 to 45 minutes.

Stout and Beef Cobbler

MAKES 1 (5-by-7-inch) savory cobbler

You know that perfect moment at the end of good bowl of stew, when you scoop up the last spoonful of meaty broth and veggies with a warm piece of bread or crumbly biscuit? That's every single bite of this cobbler. Long-simmered beef and vegetables come together with a big splash of stout and a swoon-worthy, crunchy biscuit topping for an incredibly satisfying culinary experience.

FOR THE STEW

¼ cup all-purpose flour

8 ounces stew meat, cut
   into small cubes

1 tablespoon extra-virgin olive oil

1½ cups filtered water, divided

1 tablespoon tomato paste

¼ cup diced onions

¼ cup stout, or other dark beer

½ cup sliced carrots

½ cup sliced celery

¼ teaspoon salt

¼ teaspoon dried basil

⅛ teaspoon freshly ground
   black pepper

⅛ teaspoon dried thyme

FOR THE COBBLER TOPPING

½ cup all-purpose flour

1¼ teaspoons baking powder

½ teaspoon granulated sugar

⅛ teaspoon salt

2 tablespoons cold unsalted
   butter, diced

2 tablespoons buttermilk, plus
   1 to 2 teaspoons as needed

5-by-7-inch
baking dish

PREP TIME
20 minutes

COOK TIME
2 hours, 8 minutes
to 2 hours,
10 minutes

COOLING OR
CHILLING TIME
5 to 10 minutes

SHELF LIFE
2 to 3 days

TO MAKE THE STEW

1. In a medium bowl, put the flour. Dredge the stew meat in the flour, mixing with your fingers until the meat is completely coated.

2. In a 3-quart saucepan with a lid over medium heat, heat the olive oil. Add the meat (leaving any excess flour in the bowl) and cook for 3 to 5 minutes, stirring often, until browned.

3. While the meat browns, whisk ½ cup of filtered water into the leftover flour until smooth. Set aside.

CONTINUED

4. When the meat has browned, stir in the tomato paste and onion until everything is well coated. Pour in the flour-water mixture and stir to combine.

5. Stir in the remaining 1 cup of filtered water and the stout. Bring the mixture to a low simmer and cover. Cook for 90 minutes, stirring occasionally so nothing sticks to the bottom of the pan.

6. Preheat the oven to 400°F.

7. To the stew, add the carrots, celery, salt, basil, pepper, and thyme. Simmer, uncovered, for 20 minutes. The mixture should be almost as thick as gravy. If too much liquid evaporates, add a little water, and cover the pan to finish cooking.

TO MAKE THE COBBLER TOPPING

1. While the stew simmers, in a medium bowl, whisk the flour, baking powder, sugar, and salt.

2. With a pastry blender, two knives, or your fingers, cut the butter into the flour mixture until no pieces larger than a pea remain.

3. With a fork, work in 2 tablespoons of buttermilk until a thick dough forms. Add up to 2 additional teaspoons of buttermilk, if necessary. Refrigerate the topping while the vegetables finish cooking.

4. Transfer the stew to the baking dish.

5. Remove the dough from the refrigerator. Pinch off small pieces and drop them over the stew. Continue until you have used all the dough and the top is completely covered.

6. Bake for 15 to 20 minutes until the top is golden brown.

7. Cool for 5 to 10 minutes before serving.

Ingredient Tip This recipe uses only a small portion of a can of tomato paste. To save the rest for later use, drop tablespoons of paste onto a baking sheet (that will fit in your freezer), covered with a sheet of parchment paper. Freeze for about 1 hour until solid. Once frozen, drop the balls into a freezer bag and store for up to 3 months. Use the frozen paste in stews and sauces.

5-by-7-inch
baking dish

PREP TIME
20 minutes

COOK TIME
33 to 49 minutes

COOLING OR
CHILLING TIME
5 to 10 minutes

SHELF LIFE
2 to 3 days

Chicken Cobbler

MAKES 1 (5-by-7-inch) savory cobbler

This is a fun twist on classic chicken potpie. You get creamy chicken and veggies on the bottom with drops of biscuit dough up top, rather than pie crust. I'm a big fan of this version because pie crust is delicious, but biscuit dough is also delicious and a cinch to throw together when you need some good old-fashioned comfort food in a hurry.

FOR THE COBBLER TOPPING

½ cup all-purpose flour

1¼ teaspoons baking powder

½ teaspoon granulated sugar

⅛ teaspoon salt

2 tablespoons cold unsalted butter, diced

2 tablespoons buttermilk, plus 1 to 2 teaspoons as needed

FOR THE FILLING

1 teaspoon extra-virgin olive oil

6 ounces boneless skinless chicken breast, cubed (1 cup)

½ cup sliced carrots

½ cup sliced celery

1 to 2 cups chicken broth

2 tablespoons unsalted butter

¼ cup diced onion

2 tablespoons all-purpose flour

⅓ cup milk

⅛ teaspoon salt, plus more as needed

⅛ teaspoon freshly ground black pepper, plus more as needed

TO MAKE THE COBBLER TOPPING

1. In a medium bowl, whisk the flour, baking powder, sugar, and salt.

2. With a pastry blender, two knives, or your fingers, cut the butter into the flour mixture.

3. With a fork, stir in 2 tablespoons of buttermilk to form a thick dough, adding another 1 to 2 teaspoons if necessary. Refrigerate until needed.

TO MAKE THE FILLING

1. In a 2-quart saucepan over medium heat, heat the olive oil.

2. Add the chicken and cook for 3 to 5 minutes until browned.

3. Add the carrots, celery, and enough chicken broth to cover the ingredients. Bring to a simmer and cook for 10 to 15 minutes just until the vegetables are fork tender and the chicken is cooked through.

4. When done, strain the broth into a separate container and reserve it. Set the cooked chicken and vegetable mixture aside, as well.

5. Preheat the oven to 400°F.

6. In a 1-quart saucepan over medium heat, melt the butter.

7. Add the onion and cook for 2 to 4 minutes until the edges start to become translucent.

8. Whisk in the flour until a thick paste forms and the mixture turns lightly golden.

9. Slowly whisk in the milk and ½ cup of the reserved broth. Continue to cook over medium heat for 3 to 5 minutes more, whisking constantly until the gravy is thick and bubbly. Stir in the salt and pepper, taste, and add more if necessary.

10. Transfer the chicken and vegetables to the baking dish. Top with the chicken gravy.

11. Remove the cobbler topping from the refrigerator. Crumble pieces over the top of the chicken and vegetables until the surface is covered and you have used all the topping.

12. Bake for 15 to 20 minutes until the top is golden brown.

13. Cool for 5 to 10 minutes before serving.

Variation Tip If you are a fan of peas, add ¼ cup frozen peas to the mixture when you add the carrots and celery. The same goes for frozen corn or any other favorite potpie vegetables.

Broccoli and Cheese Cobbler

MAKES 1 (5-by-7-inch) savory cobbler

5-by-7-inch
baking dish

PREP TIME
20 minutes

COOK TIME
24 to 36 minutes

COOLING OR
CHILLING TIME
5 to 10 minutes

SHELF LIFE
2 to 3 days

The last of our savory cobbler recipes takes its cue from cheesy, delicious broccoli chowder. Tender bites of broccoli and ham cooked with a rich, sharp Cheddar cheese base make for an interesting and surprising cobbler dinner. Add a pinch of cayenne pepper to the biscuit topping for a little kick of spice on top of all that cheesy goodness!

FOR THE COBBLER TOPPING

½ cup all-purpose flour

1¼ teaspoons baking powder

½ teaspoon granulated sugar

⅛ teaspoon salt

Pinch cayenne pepper (optional)

2 tablespoons cold unsalted
    butter, diced

2 tablespoons buttermilk, plus
    1 to 2 teaspoons as needed

FOR THE BROCCOLI
AND CHEESE COBBLER

1 cup chicken broth

1½ cups medium-diced broccoli

2 tablespoons unsalted butter

¼ cup diced onion

2 tablespoons all-purpose flour

½ cup milk

½ cup cubed or shredded sharp
    Cheddar cheese

¼ cup diced cooked ham

¼ teaspoon freshly ground black
    pepper, plus more as needed

⅛ teaspoon salt, plus more as needed

Preheat the oven to 400°F.

TO MAKE THE COBBLER TOPPING

1. In a medium bowl, whisk the flour, baking powder, sugar, salt, and cayenne pepper (if using).

2. With a pastry blender, two knives, or your fingers, cut the butter into the flour mixture.

3. With a fork, stir in 2 tablespoons of buttermilk to form a thick dough, adding another 1 to 2 teaspoons if necessary. Refrigerate until needed.

TO MAKE THE BROCCOLI AND CHEESE COBBLER

1. In a 2-quart saucepan over medium-high heat, bring the chicken broth to a simmer.

2. Add the broccoli, reduce the heat to medium, and cover. Cook for 4 to 7 minutes until the broccoli is fork-tender. Strain the broth into a separate container and set aside. Set the drained broccoli aside on a plate.

3. In a 1-quart saucepan over medium heat, melt the butter.

4. Add the onion and cook for 2 to 4 minutes until it starts to become translucent.

5. Whisk in the flour and cook for 1 to 2 minutes, stirring constantly, until the flour is lightly toasted. Slowly whisk in the milk and ¼ cup of the reserved cooking liquid. Cook for 2 to 3 minutes, stirring constantly, until the sauce is thick and bubbly.

6. Stir in the cooked broccoli, cheese, ham, pepper, and salt. Taste and add more salt and pepper if necessary. Pour the mixture into the baking dish.

7. Remove the topping from the refrigerator and crumble all the dough over the top until the surface is covered.

8. Bake for 15 to 20 minutes until the top is golden.

9. Cool for 5 to 10 minutes before serving.

Cooking Tip For busy weeknights, you can make the broccoli and cheese base up to 48 hours in advance. Let the base come to room temperature for about 30 minutes before baking.

Apple Cinnamon Crisp

MAKES 1 (5-by-7-inch) streusel

5-by-7-inch
baking dish

PREP TIME
10 minutes

COOK TIME
22 to 28 minutes

COOLING OR
CHILLING TIME
5 minutes

SHELF LIFE
2 to 3 days

Do you like a high ratio of crisp topping to fruit filling in your fruit crisps? If you do, you're going to love this apple cinnamon crisp. Granny Smith apples are lightly cooked with cinnamon and sugar before going into the oven under a pile of cinnamon oatmeal streusel and baked until bubbly. The crunch of the streusel with the sweet fruit is really superb.

FOR THE CRISP TOPPING

2 tablespoons all-purpose flour

2 tablespoons unsalted butter, diced

2 tablespoons quick cooking oats

2 tablespoons granulated sugar

1 tablespoon packed brown sugar

1 teaspoon ground cinnamon

FOR THE FRUIT FILLING

1 tablespoon unsalted butter

3 cups peeled and thinly sliced
Granny Smith apples

1 heaping tablespoon
granulated sugar

½ teaspoon ground cinnamon

Ice cream of choice, for serving

Preheat the oven to 400°F.

TO MAKE THE CRISP TOPPING

1. In a medium bowl, combine the flour and butter. With a pastry blender, two knives, or your fingers, cut the butter into the flour until no pieces larger than a small pea remain and crumbs begin to form.

2. Stir in the oats, granulated sugar, brown sugar, and cinnamon. Refrigerate the mixture until needed.

TO MAKE THE FRUIT FILLING

1. In a 2-quart saucepan over medium heat, melt the butter.

2. Add the apples, granulated sugar, and cinnamon. Bring to a simmer and cook for 2 to 3 minutes just until the apples are softened. Transfer the apples to the baking dish and spread them in an even layer over the bottom.

3. Remove the crisp topping from the refrigerator and sprinkle it evenly over the top.

4. Bake for 20 to 25 minutes until the fruit is bubbly.

5. Cool for 5 minutes before topping with ice cream and serving.

Cooking Tip Streusel topping can be stored in the freezer for up to 3 months. You can double the recipe and freeze half so you always have some on hand when those crisp cravings hit. Frozen streusel can be sprinkled over the fruit and put straight into the oven without thawing.

Fresh Berry Crisp

MAKES 1 (5-by-7-inch) crisp

5-by-7-inch
baking dish

PREP TIME
10 minutes

COOK TIME
20 to 30 minutes

COOLING OR
CHILLING TIME
5 minutes

SHELF LIFE
2 to 3 days

Sweet, dark berries shine when baked with a bit of sugar and lemon. The crunchy streusel with your choice of walnuts or almonds (or both—go nuts) is just the right finish on this sweet berry dessert.

FOR THE CRISP TOPPING

2 tablespoons all-purpose flour

2 tablespoons unsalted butter, diced

2 tablespoons quick cooking oats

2 tablespoons finely chopped walnuts
    or sliced almonds

2 tablespoons granulated sugar

1 tablespoon packed brown sugar

FOR THE FRUIT FILLING

2 cups fresh blueberries or
    blackberries

3 to 6 tablespoons granulated sugar

1 teaspoon cornstarch

1 teaspoon freshly squeezed
    lemon juice

¼ teaspoon grated lemon zest

Preheat the oven to 400°F.

TO MAKE THE CRISP TOPPING

1. In a small bowl, combine the flour and butter. With a pastry blender, two knives, or your fingers, cut the butter into the flour until no pieces larger than a small pea remain and crumbs begin to form.

2. Stir in the oats, walnuts, granulated sugar, and brown sugar. Refrigerate the topping until needed.

TO MAKE THE FRUIT FILLING

1. In a medium bowl, stir together the berries, granulated sugar (more or less depending on the sweetness of the berries), cornstarch, lemon juice, and lemon zest. Transfer to the baking dish.

2. Remove the crisp topping from the refrigerator and top the berries with it.

3. Bake for 20 to 30 minutes until hot and bubbly.

4. Cool for 5 minutes before serving.

Ingredient Tip You can use any type of berry for this dish. To substitute other fruits, such as peaches or apricots, increase the cornstarch to up to 1 tablespoon and reduce the sugar slightly unless your fruit is particularly tart.

Strawberry Shortcakes

baking sheet

PREP TIME
10 minutes

COOK TIME
13 to 15 minutes

COOLING OR
CHILLING TIME
10 minutes

SHELF LIFE
2 to 3 days

MAKES 4 shortcakes

For a simple summer dessert, it doesn't get better than lightly sweet short-cakes made with buttermilk under a mountain of whipped cream and fresh, juicy strawberries. Wonderfully light and easy to make, this is sure be a summertime favorite.

FOR THE SHORTCAKES

1 cup hulled, quartered strawberries

3 tablespoons granulated
    sugar, divided

1 cup all-purpose flour

2½ teaspoons baking powder

¼ teaspoon salt

4 tablespoons unsalted butter, diced

⅓ cup plus 2 tablespoons buttermilk

2 tablespoons sliced almonds

FOR THE EGG WASH

1 large egg

1 tablespoon milk

FOR THE WHIPPED CREAM

½ cup heavy (whipping) cream

1½ to 3 teaspoons granulated sugar,
    or powdered sugar

¼ teaspoon vanilla extract

1. Preheat the oven to 400°F.

2. In a small bowl, combine the strawberries and 1 tablespoon of sugar. Stir until the strawberries are well coated in sugar. Set aside and stir occasionally so the strawberries begin to release their juice.

3. Line a baking sheet with parchment paper.

4. Place a medium bowl and the electric mixer beaters (or a whisk) in the freezer.

TO MAKE THE SHORTCAKES

1. In a medium bowl, whisk the flour, baking powder, the remaining 2 tablespoons of sugar, and salt.

2. With a pastry blender, two knives, or your fingers, cut the butter into the flour mixture until no pieces larger than a pea remain.

3. With a fork, stir in the buttermilk until a thick dough forms. Divide the dough into 4 equal pieces. Pat each piece into a rough ball, and place them on the prepared sheet. Press down with the palm of your hand so each is about 1½ inches thick.

TO MAKE THE EGG WASH

1. In a small bowl, whisk the egg and milk. Brush the egg wash lightly over the shortcakes.

2. Bake the shortcakes for 13 to 15 minutes until golden.

3. Sprinkle each shortcake with ½ tablespoon of sliced almonds.

TO MAKE THE WHIPPED CREAM

1. While the shortcakes bake, remove the bowl and beaters from the freezer.

2. To the bowl, add the heavy cream, 1½ teaspoons of sugar, and the vanilla. Beat for 1 minute until well mixed, and taste. Add up to 1½ teaspoons sugar for sweeter whipped cream. Beat for 2 to 4 minutes until medium peaks form (this will take longer if whisking by hand). Refrigerate the whipped cream until you are ready to use it.

3. Remove the shortcakes from the oven and cool for at least 10 minutes before slicing in half horizontally. Top each half with whipped cream and strawberries. Serve warm or cool.

Variation Tip For a citrus twist on classic shortcakes, add ¼ teaspoon grated orange zest to the shortcake dough. Even better, replace the vanilla in the whipped cream with 2 teaspoons of Triple Sec, Grand Marnier, or freshly squeezed orange juice for orange-flavored whipped cream.

Chocolate Shortcakes

baking sheet

PREP TIME
10 minutes

COOK TIME
10 to 12 minutes

COOLING OR
CHILLING TIME
10 minutes

SHELF LIFE
2 to 3 days

MAKES 4 shortcakes

My approach to most desserts (and honestly, most things in life) is: This is great, but what if we added some chocolate? *My buttermilk shortcakes from the Strawberry Shortcakes (page 130) are great, but what if we added some chocolate? These chocolate shortcakes still have all that delicious buttermilk tang, but a deep chocolate flavor—and the sprinkling of chocolate chips throughout certainly doesn't hurt anything.*

4 tablespoons unsalted butter, diced, plus more for greasing the baking sheet

1 cup all-purpose flour

3 tablespoons natural unsweetened cocoa powder, sifted

2½ teaspoons baking powder

¼ cup granulated sugar

¼ teaspoon salt

⅓ cup semisweet chocolate chips

⅓ cup buttermilk, plus 1 tablespoon as needed

Fresh fruit of choice, for serving

Whipped Cream (page 130), for serving

1. Preheat the oven to 450°F.

2. Lightly grease a baking sheet.

3. In a medium bowl, whisk the flour, cocoa powder, baking powder, sugar, and salt.

4. With a pastry blender, two knives, or your fingers, cut the butter into the flour mixture until no pieces larger than a pea remain.

5. Add the chocolate chips and stir in the buttermilk until a thick dough forms, adding up to 1 more tablespoon of buttermilk if needed.

6. Divide the dough into 4 equal pieces, shape them into rough balls, and place them on the prepared sheet. Press down with the palm of your hand so each is about 1½ inches thick.

7. Bake for 10 to 12 minutes until the dough looks set.

8. Cool for at least 10 minutes before slicing and topping with whipped cream and fruit.

Variation Tip A drizzle of chocolate syrup makes a stellar addition. In a small saucepan over medium heat, combine 3 tablespoons water, 3 tablespoons sugar, 2 tablespoons cocoa powder, ¼ teaspoon vanilla extract, and a pinch of salt. Whisk until the ingredients come to a simmer. Simmer just until the mixture begins to thicken, and cool for 5 minutes before pouring over the filled shortcakes.

CHAPTER SIX

Cheesecakes, Puddings & Custards

Things are about to get rich and decadent because we've reached the puddings and custards stop of this little culinary journey. We will begin with three beautiful and creamy cheesecakes, mosey on through a selection of sweet and savory bread puddings, and close out the chapter with a trio of crèmes brûlées that—spoiler alert—might just be the easiest desserts in this entire book.

Tips & Techniques

Are you confused by water baths? Have trouble getting the perfect fine cookie crumb crust for your cheesecakes? Give these tips and techniques a gander. They might help clear some things up.

Using a Water Bath Recipes calling for a water bath can sound daunting, but using one is really just a matter of baking your dessert inside another pan that is partially filled with water. All you need for a water bath is a deep pan that will fit 2 (5-ounce) ramekins, and an extra pot or kettle to boil water. We will use one for all the crème brûlées, since it's an easy way to protect custards from cracking and curdling in the heat of the oven. We'll skip this extra step for the cheesecakes because these recipes are not particularly prone to cracking (and on the off chance one does, all three have toppings to cover any cracks).

Cookie Crushing The cheesecakes call for cookie and graham cracker crumb bases. The easiest way to turn cookies and crackers into fine crumbs is to process them in a food processer. If you don't own a food processor, you can make crumbs with a disposable plastic bag, a rolling pin, and a little elbow grease. Put the cookies in the bag, seal it mostly shut (leave just enough space for a little air to escape), and give the cookies a few good taps with the rolling pin to break them up. Once they are in smaller chunks, roll the pin over them until they reach a fine crumb consistency.

Testing for Doneness

For cheesecakes and crème brûlées, testing for doneness is all about visual clues. The edges should look set, but the centers should appear slightly shiny and underdone, and jiggle if gently shaken. Cheesecakes will also puff up slightly (and sink back down after baking).

For bread puddings, a knife inserted into the center should come out mostly clean. It may have streaks of custard on it, but it shouldn't be dripping with it.

Storing

All the desserts in this chapter should be covered and refrigerated. You can also freeze the cheesecakes and thaw when ready to serve. To freeze, release the cheesecake from the springform pan and place it on a plate in the freezer for 2 to 3 hours until frozen solid. Wrap tightly in aluminum foil and place it in a freezer bag. It will keep frozen for up to 2 months.

To eat, thaw in the refrigerator for 12 hours—or you can eat it frozen. Weird? No! Frozen cheesecake makes a fantastic treat on a hot day!

Torch Crème Brûlée like a Pro

Getting the perfect sugar crust on a crème brûlée can look complicated, but it's not. First sprinkle sugar over the top of the custard. Shake the ramekin until the sugar evenly coats the entire surface. Thick spots will caramelize unevenly, so take care with this step.

With a kitchen torch held 2 to 3 inches from the surface, work the flame over the sugar in small, slow circles, from the outside in. The sugar will melt and brown as you go. Stop when all the sugar is melted and the surface is nicely caramelized. Allow the sugar 2 to 3 minutes to cool and set. It's ready when you give the top a little tap with your spoon and hear a crunch.

To caramelize sugar in the oven, turn the broiler to high, give it a couple minutes to warm up, then place the ramekins on the top rack underneath the broiler element. Watch closely and rotate the dishes as necessary if they begin to brown unevenly. It should take 1 to 4 minutes (depending on the strength of your broiler) for the sugar to melt. Never walk away from dishes under the broiler. Once finished, if the custard has warmed too much in the oven, refrigerate the ramekins for 10 to 15 minutes before serving.

2 (4½-inch)
springform pans

PREP TIME
20 minutes

COOK TIME
33 to 40 minutes

COOLING OR
CHILLING TIME
3 hours, 50 minutes
to 4 hours,
15 minutes

SHELF LIFE
3 to 4 days

Dad's Birthday Cheesecake with Strawberry Glaze

MAKES 2 (4½-inch) cheesecakes

This is the dessert my dad asks for on every Father's Day and birthday, and I really can't fault his choice. It's another recipe pulled and miniaturized right out of my mom's kitchen, and I've never eaten a better classic cheesecake. It's smooth and creamy. The graham cracker base is crunchy with a touch of cinnamon, and the sour cream topping is mellow and lightly sweet. The strawberry glaze is an addition my sister and I made when we started cooking for ourselves. Now the family never serves this cheesecake without it.

FOR THE CRUST

4 whole graham cracker sheets,
    finely crushed

3 tablespoons unsalted butter,
    melted, plus more for greasing
    the springform pans

1 heaping tablespoon brown sugar

1 teaspoon ground cinnamon

Pinch salt

FOR THE CHEESECAKE FILLING

6 ounces cream cheese,
    at room temperature

¼ cup granulated sugar

1 large egg

¼ teaspoon vanilla extract

¼ teaspoon salt

FOR THE SOUR CREAM TOPPING

¾ cup sour cream

1 tablespoon granulated sugar

¼ teaspoon vanilla extract

Pinch salt

FOR THE STRAWBERRY GLAZE

½ cup water

1 pound fresh strawberries,
    medium diced, divided

¼ cup granulated sugar

1 teaspoon freshly squeezed
    lemon juice

½ tablespoon cornstarch mixed
    with 1 tablespoon water

1. Preheat the oven to 375°F.

2. Lightly grease the springform pans.

TO MAKE THE CRUST

1. In a small bowl, stir together the graham cracker crumbs, butter, brown sugar, cinnamon, and salt. Press one-third of the crumbs into the bottom of each pan. Cover the bowl containing the remaining crumbs and refrigerate for use later as topping.

2. Freeze the crusts for at least 15 minutes.

TO MAKE THE CHEESECAKE FILLING

1. In a medium bowl, whisk the cream cheese until smooth.

2. Add the granulated sugar, egg, vanilla, and salt and whisk until well combined. Pour the filling evenly into the prepared pans.

3. Bake for 15 to 20 minutes until the edges look set but the centers are still slightly jiggly. Remove from the oven and let cool for 20 to 30 minutes until the cheesecakes are room temperature.

TO MAKE THE SOUR CREAM TOPPING

1. Preheat the oven to 425°F.

2. In a small bowl, mix the sour cream, granulated sugar, vanilla, and salt. Pour evenly over the cheesecakes.

3. Bake for 3 to 5 minutes until the tops look glazed and shiny. Remove from the oven and sprinkle each with about 1 tablespoon of reserved crust crumbs.

4. Cool for 15 minutes on the counter then refrigerate for at least 3 hours before serving.

CONTINUED

TO MAKE THE STRAWBERRY GLAZE

1. In a 2-quart saucepan over medium heat, combine the water and half of the strawberries. Bring to a very low simmer and cook for 10 minutes until the strawberries are limp and the mixture is fragrant.

2. Strain the juice through a fine-mesh strainer and discard the cooked strawberries. Wipe out the saucepan and return the juice to the pan.

3. Stir in the granulated sugar, lemon juice, and cornstarch mixture. Simmer for 5 minutes until thickened. Remove from the heat and cool for 15 minutes before transferring to the refrigerator to cool completely. When the mixture is cool, stir in the remaining half of the strawberries. Spoon the glaze over the cheesecakes just before serving.

Ingredient Tip It is very important that the cream cheese be room temperature before you start, to prevent having lumps in the cheesecake. If you cannot beat the cream cheese to a smooth consistency, let it sit at room temperature for 15 minutes before trying again.

Pumpkin Cheesecake

MAKES 2 (4½-inch) cheesecakes

2 (4½-inch)
springform pans

PREP TIME
20 minutes

COOK TIME
19 to 21 minutes

COOLING OR
CHILLING TIME
3 hours, 35 minutes

SHELF LIFE
3 to 4 days

Imagine the smoothest, creamiest pumpkin pie that's ever graced your plate, add the not-so-subtle tang of cream cheese, a crunchy candy walnut topping, bump it up about 10 points on the delicious scale, and you'll have some idea of what this cheesecake tastes like. Once you try this pumpkin cheesecake, it might just replace pumpkin pie in your heart and on your Thanksgiving table.

FOR THE CRUST

3 whole graham cracker sheets,
    finely crushed

2 tablespoons unsalted butter,
    melted, plus more for greasing
    the springform pans

1 tablespoon granulated sugar

FOR THE CHEESECAKE FILLING

6 ounces cream cheese,
    at room temperature

1 large egg

¼ cup pumpkin purée

2 tablespoons heavy
    (whipping) cream

3 tablespoons granulated sugar

2 tablespoons packed brown sugar

¼ teaspoon ground cinnamon

⅛ teaspoon ground nutmeg

⅛ teaspoon ground allspice

⅛ teaspoon ground cloves

FOR THE TOPPING

⅓ cup packed brown sugar

2 tablespoons unsalted
    butter, softened

¼ cup chopped walnuts

½ cup Whipped Cream
    (page 130, half recipe)

1. Preheat the oven to 325°F.

2. Lightly grease the springform pans.

TO MAKE THE CRUST

1. In a small bowl, stir together the graham cracker crumbs, butter, and granulated sugar. Press half of the mixture into the bottom of each pan.

2. Freeze the crusts for 15 minutes.

CONTINUED

Pumpkin Cheesecake CONTINUED

TO MAKE THE CHEESECAKE FILLING

1. In a medium bowl, whisk the cream cheese until smooth.

2. Add the egg, pumpkin, heavy cream, granulated sugar, brown sugar, cinnamon, nutmeg, allspice, and cloves. Whisk until smooth and creamy. Divide the mixture evenly between the pans.

3. Bake for 14 to 16 minutes until the edges look set and the center is still slightly wobbly.

TO MAKE THE TOPPING

1. In a small bowl, stir together the brown sugar and butter until crumbly.

2. Add the walnuts and stir to combine. Sprinkle the mixture over the cheesecakes, leaving a ¼-inch space around the edges.

3. Bake for 5 minutes.

4. Remove from the oven and cool the cheesecakes on a rack for at least 20 minutes before placing them in the refrigerator. Refrigerate for at least 3 hours, or overnight. If cooling overnight, cover the pans with plastic wrap.

5. Serve topped with the whipped cream.

Cooking Tip The walnut-sugar topping will look a little oily and undercooked when it comes out of the oven. Don't worry. It will set and harden like a candy coating as the cheesecake cools.

White Chocolate Mocha Cheesecake

2 (4½-inch)
springform pans

PREP TIME
20 minutes

COOK TIME
25 to 28 minutes

COOLING OR
CHILLING TIME
3 hours, 20 minutes

SHELF LIFE
3 to 4 days

MAKES 2 (4½-inch) cheesecakes

If I'm going to pay five dollars for a sweet, sugary coffee, it's going to be a white chocolate mocha. And if I'm going to make a cheesecake for myself, it's going to be a white chocolate mocha cheesecake. This is my favorite cheesecake. It's built on a chocolate cookie base with white chocolate and espresso whipped into the cream cheese and topped with a layer of cool whipped cream, making it a perfect cheesecake imitation of my coffeehouse favorite.

FOR THE CRUST

6 Oreo cookies, finely crushed

1 tablespoon unsalted butter,
     melted, plus more for greasing
     the springform pans

FOR THE CHEESECAKE FILLING

3 ounces good-quality white
     chocolate, chopped (½ cup)

1 tablespoon heavy (whipping) cream

6 ounces cream cheese,
     at room temperature

1 large egg

⅓ cup granulated sugar

⅓ cup sour cream

½ teaspoon instant espresso granules
     dissolved in 1 tablespoon hot water

½ teaspoon vanilla extract

⅛ teaspoon salt

½ cup Whipped Cream
     (page 130, half recipe)

1. Preheat the oven to 350°F.

2. Lightly grease the springform pans.

TO MAKE THE CRUST

1. In a small bowl, stir together the cookie crumbs and butter until well mixed. Press half of the mixture into the bottom of each pan.

2. Bake for 5 minutes just until the crusts look set.

CONTINUED

TO MAKE THE CHEESECAKE FILLING

1. In a double boiler over barely simmering water, melt the white chocolate and heavy cream, stirring constantly. Remove from the heat as soon as the chocolate is mostly melted. Stir until smooth and set aside.

2. In a medium bowl, whisk the cream cheese until smooth.

3. Add the egg and sugar and whisk until well combined.

4. Whisk in the slightly cooled white chocolate until incorporated.

5. Whisk in the sour cream, dissolved espresso, vanilla, and salt until well combined. Divide the filling evenly between the pans and place them on a baking sheet.

6. Bake for 15 to 18 minutes until the edges look set but the centers are still jiggly.

7. Cool on the counter for at least 20 minutes until no longer warm to the touch. Top with the whipped cream and transfer to the refrigerator to finish chilling for at least 3 hours.

Ingredient Tip For best results, do not use inexpensive white chocolate chips for this recipe. They can be difficult to melt and won't give you the best white chocolate flavor when used as a base. If you can't find good-quality white chocolate, use regular semisweet or bittersweet chocolate instead.

Caramel Pain au Chocolat Pudding

MAKES 1 (5-by-7-inch) bread pudding

Croissants are usually a breakfast food, but this is 100 percent dessert. Buttery croissants are baked in a creamy caramel sauce and custard, with just a hint of cinnamon and vanilla, and topped with a sprinkling of chocolate chips. This is the richest, most decadent dessert in the book.

5-by-7-inch
baking dish

PREP TIME
10 minutes

COOK TIME
32 to 42 minutes

COOLING OR
CHILLING TIME
5 minutes

SHELF LIFE
1 to 2 days

Butter or shortening, for
    greasing the baking dish

3 cups cubed croissants

⅓ cup heavy (whipping) cream

⅓ cup packed brown sugar

1 large egg, lightly beaten

⅔ cup milk

2 tablespoons granulated sugar

½ teaspoon vanilla extract

½ teaspoon ground cinnamon

⅛ teaspoon salt

3 tablespoons semisweet
    chocolate chips

1. Preheat the oven to 350°F.

2. Lightly grease the baking dish. Add the croissant cubes to the dish.

3. In a 1-quart saucepan over medium heat, heat the heavy cream and brown sugar, stirring constantly, just until the sugar dissolves. Pour this over the croissants.

4. In a small bowl, lightly beat the egg.

5. Whisk in the milk, granulated sugar, vanilla, cinnamon, and salt. Pour this mixture over the croissants.

6. Sprinkle the chocolate chips over the top.

7. Bake for 30 to 40 minutes until a knife inserted into the center comes out mostly clean.

8. Cool for 5 minutes before serving.

Ingredient Tip Bakery (or homemade) croissants work better for this dish than the ones out of a can. Freeze extra croissants in a freezer bag for future bread puddings or for breakfast stratas (see chapter 8).

5-by-7-inch
baking dish

PREP TIME
20 minutes

COOK TIME
40 to 50 minutes

COOLING OR
CHILLING TIME
2 hour, 35 minutes
to 4 hours,
35 minutes

SHELF LIFE
2 to 3 days

Savory Chicken Sausage and Red Bell Pepper Bread Pudding

MAKES 1 (5-by-7-inch) savory bread pudding

Carb lovers, meet your new favorite pudding. Chicken sausage, onion, and red bell peppers are baked in a creamy custard for a rich, meaty dinner. This dish is at its best when given an hour or two to absorb the eggs and cream, but for busy evenings, you can prepare it and pop it straight into the oven for a surprisingly quick and easy dinner.

1 tablespoon unsalted butter,
    divided, plus more for greasing
    the baking dish
4 ounces chicken sausage,
    casings removed
½ cup diced red bell pepper
¼ cup diced onion
2 cups (1-inch pieces) good-quality
    white bread

½ cup grated Cheddar cheese
2 teaspoons minced fresh
    rosemary leaves
2 large eggs
½ cup milk
¼ teaspoon salt
¼ teaspoon freshly ground
    black pepper

1. Preheat the oven to 350°F.

2. Grease the baking dish.

3. In a medium pan over medium heat, melt ½ tablespoon of butter.

4. Add the sausage and cook for about 5 minutes, or until cooked through, breaking up the meat with a spatula. Transfer to a large bowl.

5. Return the pan to the heat and melt the remaining ½ tablespoon of butter. Add the red bell peppers and onion. Cook for 3 to 4 minutes until slightly softened. Stir the cooked vegetables into the sausage.

6. To the vegetables and sausage, add the bread, Cheddar cheese, and rosemary. Stir to combine, making sure the ingredients are well distributed.

7. In a medium bowl, whisk the eggs, milk, salt, and pepper. Pour this over the bread mixture and stir to combine. Pour everything into the prepared dish, cover, and refrigerate for 2 hours, or up to 4 hours. Thirty minutes before you are ready to bake it, place the dish on the counter and let it come to room temperature.

8. Bake the pudding for 30 to 40 minutes until a knife inserted into the center comes out mostly clean.

9. Cool for at least 5 minutes before serving.

Ingredient Tip This is one of those dishes great for using up leftovers. Don't have a red bell pepper? Use a green bell pepper or broccoli. No onions in your pantry, but you do have scallions? Those will work! Have some mushrooms at the end of their rope? Invite them to the party! Just give whatever you have a quick sauté before baking because the cook time is not long enough to get rid of the raw bite of anything but the softest veggies.

Vegetarian Bread Pudding

MAKES 1 (5-by-7-inch) savory bread pudding

5-by-7-inch
baking dish

PREP TIME
10 minutes

COOK TIME
40 to 50 minutes

COOLING OR
CHILLING TIME
5 minutes

SHELF LIFE
2 to 3 days

For meatless Mondays, you can't go wrong with this vegetarian bread pudding. It is rich and so hearty, packed with zucchini, tomatoes, and cheese, you won't even miss the meat! A pinch of brown sugar seems like an unusual ingredient in a savory dish, but the little hint of sweet gives all the flavors a fantastic, unexpected boost.

Butter or shortening, for greasing the baking dish

2 cups cubed French bread

1 (15-ounce) can diced tomatoes, well drained

½ cup shredded sharp Cheddar cheese, divided

½ cup chopped zucchini

1 scallion, thinly sliced

1 teaspoon packed brown sugar

1 teaspoon dried basil

¼ teaspoon dried oregano

¼ teaspoon garlic powder

2 large eggs

½ cup milk

¼ teaspoon salt

⅛ teaspoon freshly ground black pepper

¼ cup grated Parmesan cheese

1. Preheat the oven to 350°F.

2. Lightly grease the baking dish.

3. In a large bowl, combine the bread cubes, tomatoes, ¼ cup of Cheddar cheese, the zucchini, scallion, brown sugar, basil, oregano, and garlic powder. Use your hands or a large spoon to mix the ingredients well.

4. In a small bowl, whisk the eggs, milk, salt, and pepper. Pour the custard over the bread cubes, stir to combine, and transfer everything to the prepared dish.

5. Sprinkle with the remaining ¼ cup of Cheddar cheese and the Parmesan. Place the dish on a baking sheet and put into the oven.

6. Bake for 40 to 50 minutes until the top is crisp and a knife inserted into the center of the dish comes out mostly clean.

7. Cool for 5 minutes before serving.

Ingredient Tip French bread holds up well to the heft of the other ingredients, but you can also use plain white bread, or even sourdough, if that's what you have in your kitchen.

Classic Crème Brûlée

MAKES 2 crème brûlées

Need a dessert made to impress? Crème brûlée is an absolutely stunning dessert, and is secretly one of the simplest treats to make. Warmed cream, vanilla, sugar, and egg yolk magically meld together to form a rich custard. Caramelized sugar on top gives the whole thing a delicious crunchy crust. You can whip up the custard in less than 10 minutes the night before or the morning of and torch the sugar just before serving. And, if you don't have a kitchen torch, don't worry. You don't need one.

½ cup plus 2 tablespoons heavy (whipping) cream

½ teaspoon vanilla extract

3 cups boiling water

1 large egg yolk

2 tablespoons plus 2 teaspoons granulated sugar

½ teaspoon superfine sugar

1. Preheat the oven to 325°F.

2. In a small saucepan over medium heat, stir together the heavy cream and vanilla. Heat the ingredients just until they come to a simmer, then remove from the heat. Pour the cream through a fine-mesh strainer (to remove any lumpy bits) into a liquid measuring cup or container with a lip for pouring, and set aside.

3. In a medium bowl, vigorously whisk the egg yolk and granulated sugar until the mixture is a pale yellow color.

4. In a very fine stream, whisk in the warmed cream a little at a time. This brings the egg temperature up slowly so the hot cream does not scramble it. After the cream has been added to the egg mixture, whisk until well combined. Skim off any foam on top, and carefully pour the mixture into the ramekins.

Sidebar:

2 (5-ounce ramekins), deep baking pan (for the water bath)

PREP TIME
10 minutes

COOK TIME
30 to 40 minutes

COOLING OR CHILLING TIME
3 hours, 15 minutes

SHELF LIFE
1 day

5. Place the ramekins in the deep baking dish and slowly pour the boiling water around them, being careful not to splash the custards. Pour the water halfway up the sides of the ramekins.

6. Bake for 25 to 35 minutes until the edges look just set. The center will still be jiggly.

7. Remove from the oven. When cool enough to handle, remove the ramekins from the water bath. Cool on the counter for 15 minutes. Refrigerate for at least 3 hours, or up to overnight, until the custards are firm. If chilling overnight, cover the custards with plastic wrap.

8. Sprinkle the superfine sugar over each custard. With a kitchen torch, slowly melt the sugar in small, slow circles. If you don't have a kitchen torch, turn the broiler to high and place the ramekins on the top rack under the broiler element. Broil for 1 to 4 minutes, checking frequently, and rotating the ramekins as necessary. Remove from the oven when the sugar is caramelized.

Variation Tip For a lemon twist, add ½ teaspoon grated lemon zest to the cream before simmering and pour through a fine-mesh strainer to remove the zest. Stir in 1 teaspoon freshly squeezed lemon juice and prepare the rest of the recipe as written.

Chocolate Crème Brûlée

MAKES 2 crème brûlées

Just as rich and creamy as classic crème brûlée, but chocolate, so we can tack on a few extra sinfully delicious points. The dark chocolate custard can make this version a little more challenging to torch—it's not quite as clear when the sugar is going from brûlée burned to burned burned. If you've never made crème brûlée, start with Classic Crème Brûlée (page 150) to get a feel for the caramelization process. Otherwise, charge confidently onward. A magnificent chocolate experience is waiting for you.

½ cup plus 2 tablespoons heavy (whipping) cream

½ teaspoon vanilla extract

2 heaping tablespoons roughly chopped semisweet chocolate

1 large egg yolk

2 tablespoons granulated sugar

3 cups boiling water

½ teaspoon superfine sugar

1. Preheat the oven to 325°F.

2. In a 1-quart saucepan over medium heat, stir together the heavy cream and vanilla. Bring to a simmer then remove from the heat. Whisk in the chocolate until smooth. Pour the chocolate mixture through a fine-mesh strainer (to remove any lumpy bits or unmelted chocolate pieces) into a liquid measuring cup or other container with a lip for pouring, and set aside.

3. In a medium bowl, vigorously whisk the egg yolk and granulated sugar for 1 minute until the mixture is a pale yellow color.

4. Whisking constantly, very slowly pour in the chocolate mixture, giving the egg yolk time to warm so it doesn't scramble. Once all the chocolate is incorporated and the mixture is smooth, evenly divide it between the ramekins and place them in a deep baking pan.

---

2 (5-ounce ramekins), deep baking pan (for the water bath)

PREP TIME
10 minutes

COOK TIME
30 to 40 minutes

COOLING OR CHILLING TIME
3 hours, 15 minutes

SHELF LIFE
1 day

5. Pour the boiling water into the pan slowly, being careful not to splash the custards. Pour the water halfway up the sides of the ramekins.

6. Bake for 25 to 35 minutes until the sides of the custards look set but the center still jiggles.

7. Remove from the oven. When cool enough to handle, remove the ramekins from the water bath. Cool on the counter for 15 minutes. Refrigerate for at least 3 hours, or up to overnight. If chilling overnight, cover the custards with plastic wrap.

8. Sprinkle the superfine sugar over each custard. With a kitchen torch, slowly melt the sugar in small, slow circles. If you don't have a kitchen torch, turn the broiler to high and place the ramekins on the top rack under the broiler element. Broil for 1 to 4 minutes, checking frequently, and rotating the ramekins as necessary. Watch very carefully and pull from the oven as soon as the sugar looks melted.

Ingredient Tip Experiment with your favorite types of chocolate to make this crème brûlée your own.

Kahlúa Crème Brûlée

MAKES 2 crème brûlées

2 (5-ounce
ramekins), deep
baking pan (for
the water bath)

PREP TIME
10 minutes

COOK TIME
30 to 40 minutes

COOLING OR
CHILLING TIME
3 hours, 15 minutes

SHELF LIFE
1 day

As though crème brûlée isn't indulgent enough, let's make this one a little boozy too. Kahlúa is a fantastic addition to sweet dishes because, with its sweet vanilla undertones and dark rum and coffee base, it already tastes like something you'd serve for dessert. In crème brûlée, it pairs wonderfully with the richness of the creamy custard and the crunch of the burnt sugar crust.

½ cup plus 2 tablespoons
   heavy (whipping) cream

1½ teaspoons Kahlúa

½ teaspoon vanilla extract

⅛ teaspoon espresso powder

1 large egg yolk

2 tablespoons plus 2 teaspoons
   granulated sugar

3 cups boiling water

½ teaspoon superfine sugar

1. Preheat the oven to 325°F.

2. In a 1-quart saucepan, stir together the heavy cream, Kahlúa, vanilla, and espresso powder. Bring to a simmer, stirring occasionally to dissolve the espresso powder, and remove from the heat. Pour the mixture through a fine-mesh strainer (to remove any lumpy bits or undissolved espresso granules) into a liquid measuring cup or other container with a lip for pouring, and set aside.

3. In a medium bowl, vigorously whisk the egg yolk and granulated sugar until the mixture is a pale yellow color.

4. Very slowly whisk in the Kahlúa cream, giving the egg yolk time to warm so it doesn't scramble. Once the mixture is smooth, skim off any foam on top. Evenly divide the custard between the ramekins and place them in a deep baking pan.

5. Pour the boiling water around the ramekins slowly, being careful not to splash the custards. Pour the water halfway up the sides of the ramekins.

6. Bake for 25 to 35 minutes until the edges are set but the centers still jiggle.

7. Remove from the oven. When cool enough to handle, remove the ramekins from the water bath. Cool on the counter for 15 minutes. Refrigerate for 3 hours, or up to overnight. If chilling overnight, cover the custards with plastic wrap.

8. Sprinkle the superfine sugar over each custard. With a kitchen torch, slowly melt the sugar in small, slow circles. If you don't have a kitchen torch, turn the broiler to high and place the ramekins on the top rack under the broiler element. Broil for 1 to 4 minutes, checking frequently, and rotating the ramekins as necessary.

Ingredient Tip Superfine sugar is ideal for topping crème brûlée because it melts quickly and easily. It can be found in most grocery stores in the baking aisle, or you can make your own by running regular granulated sugar through the food processor for a few seconds.

CHAPTER SEVEN

Pies & Tarts

This chapter is packed with everything from classic fruit pies to stunning little breakfast tarts. Get out your rolling pin, flour up those hands, and put on an apron because this one's going to get a little messy—but oh, the things we'll make along the way.

Tips & Techniques

Pie baking can feel intimidating, but once you get the basics down, it's the most fun you'll have in the kitchen. Here are a few techniques and tips you might find helpful.

Blind Baking This means baking a crust without a filling. It's not as scary as it sounds. First, cover your unbaked pie crust or tart crust with aluminum foil or parchment paper, then fill the crust with pie weights to weigh it down, and finally prebake it before filling. Blind baking ensures a fully cooked crust every time, and is used with custard pies and other fillings that don't require enough oven time for the crust to bake all the way through.

Pie Weight Alternatives You need pie weights for blind baking. You can buy a set, or use about 1 cup of dried beans or uncooked rice. You can't use the beans or rice in any recipes afterward, so store them in a labeled Mason jar or plastic bag to reuse as pie weights.

Fluting Fluting is an attractive way to finish the edges of your pie. The simplest fluting method is to use your left-hand index finger on the inside of the pie to push the dough between the second knuckles of your right-hand index and middle fingers on the outside, making a U shape. Repeat all the way around the pie. If you come to a thin spot, patch it with scrap dough and a bit of water.

Pie Serving Size Like most desserts in this book, these pies yield 2 to 4 servings—4 for small eaters and 2 for bigger appetites. Plan on half a pie per person, especially if you want leftovers.

How to Make a Lattice Top

A lattice top makes a lovely finish to a fruit pie, and is actually much easier than it looks. Once you roll out your dough, use a pizza cutter or long chef's knife to cut ½-inch-thick strips, or as thin as you feel comfortable working with (the thinner the strips, the more weaving you do).

1. Lay half of the strips vertically across the pie, leaving a strip's width between each.
2. Working on one side of the pie, peel back alternating pieces of dough just to the center of the pie.
3. Drape a strip of dough crosswise over the remaining strips, close to the center.
4. Lay the peeled-back pieces back down.
5. Now peel back the other strips and lay down another piece of dough.
6. Repeat until you finish that side. Turn the pie around and repeat with the other half. Work quickly but carefully, and if any pieces tear, just pinch them back together with a couple drops of water to help the pieces stick.
7. To finish the edges, trim any pieces longer than the overhang on the bottom crust and fold the strips and the bottom crust under so they sit on the lip of the pie pan. Flute the edge if you'd like or bake as is.

Testing for Doneness

Using visual clues for doneness, look for bubbly fruit and a golden crust. Fruit pies need both to be considered done.

For the pastries, hand pies, and tarts with baked fillings, look for a pretty golden crust so you know it is cooked through, crispy, and ready to eat.

Storing

Fruit pies and hand pies can be stored loosely covered at room temperature for up to 2 days. The custard/pudding pies, all tarts, and the hand pies and pastries containing meat or egg filling, should be wrapped and refrigerated. Some people prefer to make fruit pies in stages, so use the following cheat sheet for pie storage at any stage.

PIE TYPE	REFRIGERATOR STORAGE	FREEZER STORAGE
Unbaked pie dough disks or dough shaped in a pie pan	Store tightly wrapped in plastic wrap; use within 48 hours	Tightly wrap in plastic wrap and place in a freezer bag; will keep for 2 months; no need to thaw before filling and baking.
Filled, unbaked pies	Do not refrigerate for any length of time because the bottoms become soggy.	Tightly wrap in plastic wrap or aluminum foil and place in a freezer bag; will keep for 2 months. To bake, bake as directed in the recipe but add 20 to 30 minutes more to the baking time.
Leftover pie	Store wrapped in plastic wrap or in an airtight container for 3 to 4 days.	Freeze solid on a plate, wrap tightly in plastic wrap or aluminum foil, and place in a freezer bag; will keep for 2 months. Thaw on the counter for 1 hour, or in the refrigerator for 12 hours, before reheating.

All-Butter Buttermilk Pie Crust

MAKES 1 double or 1 single pie crust; 2 or 4 (4¾-inch) round tart shells

This my favorite pie crust. It's flaky and delicious and easy to make, and best of all, it's very easy to work with. For hand pies and tarts and anything that requires me to work with the dough longer than simply rolling it out, this is my go-to pie crust. The one drawback is that as an all-butter crust, it doesn't hold up to heat in the oven as well as crusts made with shortening. So, if you want fancy fluting or perfect cut-outs, look elsewhere (like the equally delicious Basic Flaky Pie Crust on page 164).

6-inch pie pan or 2 (4¾-inch) tart pans

PREP TIME
10 minutes

COOK TIME
15 to 20 minutes for the crusts;
12 to 13 minutes for the tart shells

COOLING OR CHILLING TIME
1 hour, 30 minutes

SHELF LIFE
2 days

FOR A DOUBLE CRUST OR 4 (4¾-INCH) TART SHELLS

8 tablespoons unsalted butter, cut into ½-inch chunks

1¼ cups all-purpose flour, plus more for flouring the work surface and the rolling pin

2 teaspoons granulated sugar

½ teaspoon salt

¼ cup buttermilk

FOR A SINGLE CRUST OR 2 (4¾-INCH) TART SHELLS

4 tablespoons unsalted butter, cut into ½-inch chunks

½ cup plus 2 tablespoons all-purpose flour, plus more for flouring the work surface and the rolling pin

1 teaspoon granulated sugar

¼ teaspoon salt

2 tablespoons buttermilk

TO MAKE THE CRUST

1. Place the butter in the freezer for 15 minutes before you plan to begin.

2. In a medium bowl, whisk the flour, sugar, and salt.

3. If using a food processor: Transfer the flour mixture to a food processor. Add the butter and pulse until it is cut into the flour and no pieces larger than a pea remain. Slowly pulse in the buttermilk until the mixture just begins to clump. If using a pastry blender: Add the butter to the flour mixture. With a pastry blender, two knives, or your fingers, cut the butter into the flour until no pieces larger than a pea remain. With a fork, slowly stir the buttermilk into the flour until a thick dough forms.

CONTINUED

4. The dough will look rough and crumbly. If you squeeze a handful together and it holds its shape, it's ready (if not, drizzle in 1 to 2 teaspoons buttermilk, and continue to process until it does).

5. If making a double crust, divide the dough in half, form it into 2 disks, and wrap each tightly in plastic wrap. Otherwise, wrap all the dough. Refrigerate for at least 45 minutes.

TO BLIND BAKE A SINGLE CRUST (FOR CUSTARD PIES AND QUICHES)

1. Let the chilled dough sit at room temperature for about 5 minutes until slightly softened.

2. On a well-floured surface and with a floured rolling pin, roll out the dough to an ⅛-inch thickness and drape it over the pie pan. Using kitchen scissors or a knife, trim the excess dough, leaving a 1-inch overhang. Fold the excess dough under to create a lip all the way around the pie and flute, if desired. Place the dough in the freezer for 30 minutes.

3. Preheat the oven to 425°F.

4. Place a sheet of aluminum foil or parchment paper just over the inside of the crust. Fill the pie with pie weights, dried beans, or rice. This will keep the crust from puffing up as it bakes. Bake for 12 to 15 minutes until the edges just turn golden. Remove the foil and the weights and bake the crust for 3 to 5 minutes just until the bottom looks dry. Remove from the oven. If the bottom has puffed at all, gently pat it down.

TO BLIND BAKE 2 TART SHELLS

1. Preheat the oven to 400°F.

2. Divide the dough in half. On a well-floured surface and with a floured rolling pin, roll out half the dough thinly enough so there is at least 1 inch of dough around the tart pan when placed on top of the dough. Drape the dough into the tart pan and gently press it down to the bottom and the sides for a tight fit. Run the rolling pin gently over the top to cut off excess dough. Repeat with the remaining dough.

3. Place both tart pans on a baking sheet and cover each with a piece of parchment paper. Fill the tarts with pie weights, or dried beans, or rice and bake for 10 minutes. Remove the parchment paper and the weights and bake for 2 to 3 minutes just until the bottoms look dry and the edges are very lightly golden. If the bottom has puffed up at all, gently pat it down.

Cooking Tip You can use this blind baking method on the Basic Flaky Pie Crust (page 164), as well.

6-inch pie pan

PREP TIME
10 minutes

COOK TIME
0 minutes

COOLING OR
CHILLING TIME
45 minutes

SHELF LIFE
2 days

Basic Flaky Pie Crust

MAKES 1 double or 1 single pie crust

The crust is the foundation upon which a pie is built. You want to make sure it's a good one—and this most definitely is. Tender and flaky, sprinkle a little sugar on it and this crust could be a satisfying dessert all on its own. A mixture of butter and shortening ensures you get a rich, buttery crust that will hold up to the heat of the oven so your beautiful fluting stays beautiful; the vinegar helps keep it extra flaky. You can make this crust in a food processor or by hand with a pastry blender. There are instructions for both methods.

FOR A DOUBLE CRUST

6 tablespoons unsalted butter,
    cut into ½-inch chunks

3 tablespoons vegetable shortening

1½ cups all-purpose flour

1 tablespoon granulated sugar

¼ teaspoon salt

½ teaspoon apple cider vinegar

¼ cup ice-cold water, plus
    1 tablespoon as needed

FOR A SINGLE CRUST

3 tablespoons unsalted butter,
    cut into ½-inch chunks

1 tablespoon plus 1½ teaspoons
    vegetable shortening

¾ cup all-purpose flour

1½ teaspoons granulated sugar

⅛ teaspoon salt

¼ teaspoon apple cider vinegar

2 tablespoons ice-cold water, plus
    1½ teaspoons as needed

1. Place the butter and shortening in the freezer 15 minutes before you plan to begin. Cold ingredients are much easier to work with.

2. In a medium bowl, whisk the flour, sugar, and salt.

3. If using a food processor: Transfer the flour mixture to a food processor. Add the very cold butter and shortening and pulse until they are cut into the flour and no pieces larger than a pea remain. Stir the apple cider into the ice water. Drizzle the liquid into the processor and pulse just until the dough begins to clump. If using a pastry blender: Add the butter and shortening to the flour mixture.With a pastry blender, two knives, or your fingers, cut them into the flour until no pieces larger than a pea remain. Stir the apple cider vinegar into the ice water and slowly drizzle the liquid into the bowl, stirring with a fork. Continue to stir until a thick dough forms.

4. Add more ice water by the ½ teaspoon if needed, up to 1 tablespoon (1½ teaspoons for a single crust).

5. If making a double crust, divide the dough in half, form it into 2 disks, and wrap each tightly in plastic wrap. Otherwise, wrap all the dough. Refrigerate for 30 minutes before rolling.

Cooking Tip Make sure to measure the flour correctly. If you don't have a kitchen scale, use the scoop and sweep method (see bottom of page 19). Too much flour can prevent the dough from coming together.

Classic Apple Pie

MAKES 1 (6-inch) pie

6-inch pie pan

PREP TIME
20 minutes

COOK TIME
50 minutes to
1 hour

COOLING OR
CHILLING TIME
2 hours, 30 minutes

SHELF LIFE
3 to 4 days

The best apple pies are often the simplest and it doesn't get much simpler than this. Granny Smith apples are simmered in a mixture of butter, cinnamon, and sugar and piled into a classic flaky crust. When the pie comes out of the oven, it's beautiful and golden and simply packed full of tart apples—and all that butter and sugar caramelize to make the most gooey, amazing filling you've ever eaten. Ice cream on the side is a must, and if you want to grate a little Cheddar cheese over the pie while it's still warm, no one is going to stop you.

1 tablespoon all-purpose flour, plus more for flouring the work surface and the rolling pin

1 recipe Basic Flaky Pie Crust for a double crust (page 164), chilled

1 large egg white, whisked until foamy

2 tablespoons unsalted butter

5 cups thinly sliced Granny Smith apples (3 to 4 large apples)

3 tablespoons packed brown sugar

2 tablespoons granulated sugar

½ teaspoon ground cinnamon

½ teaspoon vanilla extract

¼ teaspoon ground nutmeg

¼ teaspoon salt

1 large egg

1 tablespoon milk

1. On a well-floured surface and with a floured rolling pin, roll out the first disk of dough and drape it over the pie pan. Gently press the dough into the bottom and sides of the pan for a tight fit. Trim the edges, leaving a ½-inch overhang. Brush the bottom lightly with egg white (this will help prevent a soggy crust), and refrigerate the crust for at least 15 minutes.

2. In a 2-quart pot over medium heat, melt the butter. Add the apples, brown sugar, granulated sugar, cinnamon, vanilla, nutmeg, and salt. Bring to a simmer and cook for 5 to 6 minutes, stirring frequently, until the apples are tender.

3. Stir in the flour. Remove from the heat and set aside to cool for 15 minutes.

4. Preheat the oven to 425°F.

5. Place a baking sheet in the oven (if using a glass or ceramic pie pan, skip this step because the preheated sheet can cause the pan to shatter).

6. Remove the crust from the refrigerator and fill it with the apple mixture, piling the apples highest in the center.

7. On a well-floured surface and with a floured rolling pin, roll out the top crust. Drape this over the pie and gently press the dough into the bottom and sides of the pan for a tight fit. Trim the edges, leaving a ½-inch overhang. Fold the edges under and flute or crimp with a fork to seal.

8. In a small bowl, whisk the egg and milk. Brush the egg wash over the top of the pie. With a sharp knife, cut 4 slits in the top crust for steam to escape.

9. Place the pie on the baking sheet and bake for 15 minutes.

10. Reduce the heat to 350°F and bake for 30 to 40 minutes until the crust is golden and the filling is bubbling. If the crust becomes too brown, cover it with aluminum foil to prevent burning.

11. Cool at room temperature for at least 2 hours before serving.

Ingredient Tip Mix and match your apples if you like. Honeycrisps are a great but expensive baking apple. Golden Delicious and Braeburns are popular as well (no Red Delicious, please). If using sweet apples, add a squeeze of fresh lemon juice to the mix or use a mixture of sweet and tart apples for a pie with a more complex flavor.

Pumpkin Pie

MAKES 1 (6-inch) pie

6-inch pie pan

PREP TIME
20 minutes

COOK TIME
35 to 45 minutes

COOLING OR
CHILLING TIME
4 hours,
20 minutes

SHELF LIFE
3 to 4 days

For intimate Thanksgiving gatherings or preholiday pie cravings, this little pumpkin pie is perfect. Most pumpkin pie recipes use evaporated milk, but for small-batch baking I have trouble finding uses for the leftover milk. So this pie uses heavy cream instead. It gives the pie a rich, smooth texture that is incredibly appealing. Not too sweet and just lightly spiced, you might find yourself hoarding the leftovers.

1 recipe All-Butter Buttermilk Pie
   Crust for a single crust (page 161),
   blind baked (see page 162)
½ cup heavy (whipping) cream
½ cup canned pumpkin purée
¼ cup packed brown sugar
1 large egg yolk

2 teaspoons molasses (optional)
½ teaspoon ground cinnamon
¼ teaspoon salt
⅛ teaspoon ground ginger
⅛ teaspoon ground nutmeg
Pinch ground cloves
Whipped Cream (page 130)

1. Preheat the oven to 400°F.

2. Have the prepared pie crust ready.

3. In a bowl, combine the heavy cream, pumpkin, brown sugar, egg yolk, molasses (if using), cinnamon, salt, ginger, nutmeg, and cloves. Whisk until smooth and pour into the prepared crust. Smooth the top and place in the oven.

4. Immediately reduce the temperature to 350°F. Bake for 35 to 45 minutes until the top looks set but the center is still a little jiggly. Keep a close eye on the crust. If it becomes too browned, cover it with aluminum foil to keep it from burning.

5. Cool the pie on the counter for 20 minutes. Refrigerate for at least 4 hours. Serve topped with whipped cream.

Ingredient Tip The molasses gives this pie a slightly darker, richer taste, but if you prefer the taste of classic pumpkin pie, omit it!

Cherry Pie

MAKES 1 (6-inch) pie

6-inch pie pan

PREP TIME
30 minutes

COOK TIME
42 to 52 minutes

COOLING OR
CHILLING TIME
3 hours, 15 minutes

SHELF LIFE
3 to 4 days

Ask any baker and they'll tell you the worst part about making cherry pie is pitting all those cherries. The bad news first: You will have to pit some cherries for this pie. The good news: It's a mini pie, so not nearly as many and it is totally worth it. A touch of almond extract brings out the tart and sweet flavor of the cherry filling. Once cooked, the cherries become thick and syrupy but still maintain their shape and texture. As you anticipate the first bite, know you'll get that amazing sensation unique to cherry pie— the cherries bursting over your tongue.

All-purpose flour, for flouring the work surface and the rolling pin

1 recipe All-Butter Buttermilk Pie Crust for a double crust (page 161)

1 large egg white, beaten until frothy

2 cups pitted sweet cherries

½ cup granulated sugar

2 tablespoons cornstarch

2 teaspoons freshly squeezed lemon juice

¼ teaspoon salt

¼ teaspoon almond extract

1 large egg

1 tablespoon milk

1. On a well-floured surface and with a floured rolling pin, roll out the bottom crust and drape it over the pie pan. Gently press the dough into the bottom and sides of the pan for a tight fit. Trim the edges, leaving a ½-inch overhang. Brush the bottom and sides with a thin layer of egg white. Refrigerate while you prepare the filling.

2. In a 2-quart saucepan, stir together the cherries, sugar, cornstarch, lemon juice, salt, and almond extract. Bring to a simmer and cook for 2 minutes. Set aside to cool for about 15 minutes until the cherries are no longer hot to the touch.

CONTINUED

3. Preheat the oven to 425°F.

4. On a well-floured surface and with a floured rolling pin, roll out the top pie crust.

5. Fill the pie with the cooled cherries and drape the top crust over the pie. Trim the edges and roll them under. Crimp with a fork, if desired.

6. Whisk the egg and milk and brush the egg wash over the pie. Cut 4 slits in the top of the pie for steam to escape.

7. Bake for 15 minutes at 425°F, then lower the temperature to 350°F and bake 25 to 35 minutes until the crust is golden and the filling is bubbling. Cover the pie with aluminum foil if the top begins to brown too quickly.

8. Cool completely, at least 3 hours, before cutting and serving.

Ingredient Tip Almond extract is a classic addition to cherry pie, but if you don't like the flavor, replace it with ½ teaspoon vanilla extract.

Chocolate Pudding Pie

MAKES 1 (6-inch) pie

No way were we getting through this chapter without at least one recipe containing chocolate. Chocolate Pudding Pie is so easy it's almost criminal. The base is made with crushed Oreo cookies and the filling comes together in about 10 minutes. Then you pile on some whipped cream, add a few chocolate shavings, and try not to wear a hole in the floor while you wait for the pie to set.

2 tablespoons melted unsalted butter, 1 tablespoon unsalted butter, unmelted, plus more for greasing the pie pan

10 Oreo cookies, finely crushed

¼ cup plus 2 tablespoons granulated sugar

1 tablespoon cornstarch

Pinch salt

¾ cup milk (whole milk preferred)

1 large egg yolk

⅓ cup chopped bittersweet chocolate, plus more for garnish

¼ teaspoon vanilla extract

½ cup Whipped Cream (page 130, half recipe)

1. Preheat the oven to 350°F.

2. Lightly grease the pie pan.

3. In a small bowl, stir together the cookie crumbs and 2 tablespoons of melted butter until the mixture begins to clump. Transfer the crumbs to the pie pan and firmly press and spread the mixture out until it covers the bottom and sides of the pan.

CONTINUED

6-inch pie pan

PREP TIME
10 minutes

COOK TIME
12 to 14 minutes

COOLING OR
CHILLING TIME
4 hours

SHELF LIFE
3 to 4 days

Chocolate Pudding Pie CONTINUED

4. Bake for 7 to 9 minutes until the crust looks set. Remove from the oven and cool completely.

5. In a 2-quart saucepan over low-medium heat, combine the sugar, cornstarch, and salt.

6. Slowly whisk in the milk and egg yolk until well combined. Cook for about 5 minutes until thick and bubbles begin to form around the edges. Remove from the heat and stir in the chocolate, the remaining 1 tablespoon of butter, and the vanilla, until completely smooth.

7. If there are any lumps in the pudding, pour it through a fine-mesh strainer, using a whisk to press the pudding through. Otherwise, pour it directly into the cooled crust. Refrigerate for at least 4 hours.

8. Top with whipped cream and chopped chocolate.

Cooking Tip You can make fancy chocolate curls for garnishing with a chocolate bar and a vegetable peeler. Run the peeler down the edge of the chocolate bar to create the curl. Use the long sides of the chocolate bar for large curls or the short sides for smaller ones.

Fresh Berry Galette

MAKES 1 (6-inch) galette

Galettes are fruit pies' less-fussy cousins. They are really the best of both worlds. While incredibly easy to make, their appearance is so simple and rustic that it somehow manages to look almost fancy. When you pull one of these out of the oven, people are almost always intrigued and impressed. This berry version is positively drool-worthy. Dark berries cooked with a bit of sugar become thick and bubbly when baked inside the buttermilk crust, making a simply beautiful dessert.

1 recipe All-Butter Buttermilk Pie Crust for a single crust (page 161)

1 cup fresh blackberries, blueberries, or a mixture

1 peach, peeled and cut into ½-inch slices (optional)

2 to 3 tablespoons granulated sugar, plus more for sprinkling the crust

½ teaspoon cornstarch

1 teaspoon freshly squeezed lemon juice

All-purpose flour, for flouring the work surface and the rolling pin

1 teaspoon unsalted butter, diced

1 large egg

1 tablespoon milk

Ice cream of choice, for serving

baking sheet

PREP TIME
15 minutes

COOK TIME
25 to 35 minutes

COOLING OR
CHILLING TIME
15 minutes

SHELF LIFE
2 to 3 days

1. Let the chilled dough sit at room temperature for 10 to 15 minutes just until softened but the butter in the dough is not overly softened.

2. Preheat the oven to 400°F.

3. Line a baking sheet with parchment paper.

4. In a medium bowl, stir together the berries, peach slices (if using), sugar (more or less depending on how sweet the berries are), cornstarch, and lemon juice until well mixed. Set aside.

CONTINUED

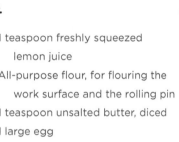

5. Generously flour the work surface and a rolling pin. Use as much flour over and under the dough as needed to keep it from sticking and lift and turn the dough a quarter turn after every other roll so you get as even a circle as possible. Roll out the dough to a ⅛-inch thickness. Proper dough thickness will make folding easier, so use a ruler if you aren't sure. Place the dough in the center of the prepared sheet.

6. Pile the berry filling in the center, leaving a 1½-inch border. In 5 or 6 folds (more if you need it), fold the edges of the dough up so the fruit is enclosed. Galettes are meant to be rustic so if some folds don't look perfect, don't worry. Dot the top of the fruit evenly with the butter.

7. In a small bowl, whisk the egg and milk and brush the egg wash lightly over the dough, getting it into the folds and pressing them back together. Sprinkle the crust lightly with sugar.

8. Bake for 25 to 35 minutes until the fruit is bubbling and the crust is golden.

9. Cool for 15 minutes before slicing and serving with ice cream.

Ingredient Tip The butter helps give the baked fruit a glossy sheen. You need just enough to dot the exposed surface of the fruit. If you have leftover galette, the butter may cool and harden, making the top look dull, but it will return to its liquid state as soon as you reheat the leftovers.

Strawberry and Lemon Galette

MAKES 1 (6-inch) galette

Sweet strawberries and a little lemon zest make this galette, with its golden sugared crust, a perfect summer pastry. I can't fully put into words how delightfully easy to make and wonderfully fresh tasting this dessert is. You should experience it for yourself.

1 recipe All-Butter Buttermilk Pie
    Crust for a single crust (page 161)

1 cup sliced fresh strawberries

2 tablespoons granulated sugar, plus
    more for sprinkling the crust

½ teaspoon cornstarch

1 teaspoon freshly squeezed
    lemon juice

¼ teaspoon grated lemon zest

All-purpose flour, for flouring the
    work surface and the rolling pin

1 teaspoon unsalted butter, diced

1 large egg

1 tablespoon milk

Ice cream of choice, for serving

baking sheet

PREP TIME
15 minutes

COOK TIME
25 to 35 minutes

COOLING OR
CHILLING TIME
15 minutes

SHELF LIFE
2 to 3 days

1. Let the chilled pie crust dough sit on the counter for 10 to 15 minutes just until softened but the butter in the dough is not overly softened.

2. Preheat the oven to 400°F.

3. Line a baking sheet with parchment paper.

4. In a medium bowl, stir together the strawberries, sugar, cornstarch, lemon juice, and lemon zest until well mixed. Set aside.

5. Generously flour the work surface and a rolling pin. Use as much flour over and under the dough as needed to keep it from sticking and lift and turn the dough a quarter turn after every other roll so you get as even a circle as possible. Roll out the dough to a ⅛-inch thickness. Proper dough thickness will make folding easier, so use a ruler if you aren't sure. Place the dough in the middle of the prepared sheet.

CONTINUED

6. Pile the strawberries in the center of the crust, leaving a 1½-inch border. In 5 or 6 folds (more if you need it), fold the edges of the dough up so the fruit is enclosed. Galettes are meant to be rustic so if some folds don't look perfect, don't worry. Dot the top of the fruit evenly with the butter.

7. In a small bowl, whisk the egg and milk. Brush the egg wash over the crust, especially in the folds, then lightly sprinkle the crust with sugar.

8. Bake for 25 to 35 minutes until the crust is deeply golden and the fruit is bubbling.

9. Cool for 15 minutes before slicing and serving with ice cream.

Ingredient Tip The lemon flavor is very present in this galette; it's not just there as a flavor booster. If you don't like lemon, omit the zest. The juice alone with help bring out the strawberry flavor without overwhelming it.

Maple Brown Sugar Pastries

baking sheet

PREP TIME
20 minutes

COOK TIME
14 to 16 minutes

COOLING OR
CHILLING TIME
10 to 20 minutes

SHELF LIFE
3 to 4 days

MAKES 4 pastries

You know those toasted pastries that come wrapped in foil that we all loved as kids? They weren't allowed in my house growing up so, of course, they were the holy grail of breakfast foods for 10-year-old me. As an adult, I've replaced them in my affections with this homemade version of flaky buttermilk pie crust stuffed with a brown sugar and cinnamon mixture and covered with maple glaze. The best part is I can make these any time I want.

FOR THE CRUST

All-purpose flour, for flouring the
    work surface and the rolling pin
1 recipe All-Butter Buttermilk Pie
    Crust for a double crust (page 161)

FOR THE FILLING

3 tablespoons packed brown sugar
1½ teaspoons all-purpose flour
½ teaspoon ground cinnamon

FOR THE EGG WASH

1 large egg
1 tablespoon milk

FOR THE MAPLE GLAZE

½ cup powdered sugar, sifted
1 to 2 teaspoons milk
½ teaspoon ground cinnamon
¼ teaspoon vanilla extract
⅛ teaspoon maple extract

1. Preheat the oven to 425°F.

2. Line a baking sheet with parchment paper.

TO MAKE THE CRUST

On a well-floured work surface and with a floured rolling pin, roll out the dough to an 8-by-10-inch rectangle, ¼ inch thick. With a ruler and a pizza cutter, trim the edges so they're even and cut the rectangle into 8 (2½-by-4-inch) rectangles. Gather up the scraps, roll, and cut again if needed. Place the rectangles on the prepared sheet and refrigerate while you make the filling.

CONTINUED

TO MAKE THE FILLING

In a small bowl, stir together the brown sugar, flour, and cinnamon.

TO MAKE THE EGG WASH

In another small bowl, whisk the egg and milk. Brush the egg wash over the tops of the rectangles.

TO ASSEMBLE THE PASTRIES

1. Spread 1 scant tablespoon of filling over 4 rectangles, leaving a ½-inch border.

2. Top with the remaining rectangles, egg wash–side down. Use a fork to crimp the edges closed all the way around. Brush egg wash over the tops and poke each pastry 4 or 5 times with the tines of a fork to create holes for steam to escape.

3. Bake for 14 to 16 minutes until golden.

4. Cool on the baking sheet for 5 to 10 minutes before glazing.

TO MAKE THE MAPLE GLAZE

1. In a medium bowl, whisk the powdered sugar, 1 teaspoon of milk, the cinnamon, vanilla, and maple extract. Add up to 1 teaspoon of milk until the glaze reaches the desired consistency.

2. Spoon the glaze over the pastries and let them sit for 5 to 10 minutes for the glaze to set.

Ingredient Tip You can omit the maple extract if you don't have any. They won't be *Maple* Brown Sugar Pastries, but they will still be delicious.

baking sheet

PREP TIME
20 minutes

COOK TIME
14 to 16 minutes

COOLING OR
CHILLING TIME
10 to 15 minutes

SHELF LIFE
3 to 4 days

Jam Pastries with Butter and Vanilla Glaze

MAKES 4 pastries

This jam variation on my Maple Brown Sugar Pastries (page 177) is even simpler than its brown sugar sibling. A healthy spoonful of your favorite jam makes a perfect bubbly filling for these breakfast treats. Whisk together a quick butter and vanilla glaze, top with sprinkles, and you have a morning meal your inner child will love.

FOR THE CRUST

All-purpose flour, for flouring the
    work surface and the rolling pin
1 recipe All-Butter Buttermilk Pie
    Crust for a double crust (page 161)

FOR THE EGG WASH

1 large egg
1 tablespoon milk

FOR THE FILLING

4 tablespoons thick jam of choice

FOR THE GLAZE

½ cup powdered sugar, sifted
½ tablespoon unsalted butter, melted
1 to 2 teaspoons milk
⅛ teaspoon vanilla extract
Pinch salt
Sprinkles, for decorating

1. Preheat the oven to 425°F.

2. Line a baking sheet with parchment paper.

TO MAKE THE CRUST

Flour the work surface and a rolling pin. Roll out the dough to an 8-by-10-inch rectangle, ¼ inch thick. With a pizza cutter and ruler, trim the edges so they're even, then cut the rectangle into 8 (2½-by-4-inch) rectangles. Gather up the scraps, roll, and cut again if needed. Transfer the rectangles to the prepared sheet, using a spatula if the dough is sticking.

TO MAKE THE EGG WASH

In a small bowl, whisk the egg and milk. Brush the egg wash over the tops
of the rectangles.

TO ASSEMBLE THE PASTRIES

1. Spoon 1 tablespoon of jam over 4 rectangles.

2. Top with the remaining rectangles, egg wash–side down. Use a fork to
crimp the edges closed all the way around. Brush egg wash over the tops
and poke each pastry 4 or 5 times with the tines of a fork to create holes
for steam to escape.

3. Bake for 14 to 16 minutes until golden.

4. Cool for 5 to 10 minutes before making the glaze.

TO MAKE THE GLAZE

1. In a small bowl, whisk the powdered sugar, butter, milk, vanilla, and salt.

2. Spoon the glaze over the pastries.

3. Add a generous coating of sprinkles while the glaze is still wet. Let the
glaze set for 5 minutes before eating.

Ingredient Tip Thick jams work better in these pastries than thin jellies,
which can seep out while baking. Crimp the edges well to prevent any filling
from escaping.

baking sheet

PREP TIME
20 minutes

COOK TIME
18 to 22 minutes

COOLING OR
CHILLING TIME
5 minutes

SHELF LIFE
3 to 4 days

Savory Breakfast Pastries

MAKES 4 pastries

My trio of breakfast pastries wouldn't be complete without a savory addition. This one is a tasty cheese scramble with ham and scallions wrapped in pastry, brushed with an egg wash, and baked until golden and beautiful. This recipe makes four pastries, and I recommend putting some away before you start eating yours, because you won't want to stop at just one!

2 large eggs

2 tablespoons milk

Cooking spray

¼ cup finely diced cooked ham

1 tablespoon finely diced scallion

All-purpose flour, for flouring the work surface and rolling pin

1 recipe All-Butter Buttermilk Pie Crust for a double crust (page 161)

4 tablespoons shredded sharp Cheddar cheese

1. Preheat the oven to 425°F.

2. Line a baking sheet with parchment paper.

3. In a small bowl, whisk the eggs and milk and set aside.

4. Spray a small skillet with cooking spray and place it over medium heat.

5. Add the ham and scallion and cook for 3 to 5 minutes until the ham looks browned and the scallion is slightly softened.

6. Reserve 2 tablespoons of egg mixture to use as egg wash, and pour the remaining eggs into the skillet. Scramble the eggs to your desired doneness and set aside.

7. On a well-floured surface and with a floured rolling pin, roll out the dough to an 8-by-10-inch rectangle, ¼ inch thick. With a pizza cutter and a ruler, trim the edges so they're even, then cut the rectangle into 8 (2½-by-4-inch) rectangles. Transfer the pieces to the prepared sheet.

8. Brush the rectangles with egg wash.

9. Evenly divide the eggs and ham among 4 rectangles, leaving at least a ½-inch border. Sprinkle each with 1 tablespoon of Cheddar cheese. Top with the remaining rectangles, egg wash–side down. Use a fork to crimp the edges closed all the way around. Brush egg wash over the tops and poke each pastry 4 or 5 times with the tines of a fork to create holes for steam to escape.

10. Bake for 12 to 14 minutes until the pastries are golden.

11. Cool for 5 minutes before serving.

Cooking Tip If you have too much filling in the pastries for the top piece of dough to fit over it, very carefully stretch the dough so it is slightly larger than the bottom piece, and it should fit just fine. If any pieces tear or break, rub a drop or two of water over the edges and press them back together.

Gruyère Apple Hand Pies

MAKES 5 small hand pies

baking sheet

PREP TIME
20 minutes

COOK TIME
18 to 22 minutes

COOLING OR
CHILLING TIME
20 minutes

SHELF LIFE
3 to 4 days

Years ago, I watched a character on a television show grate Gruyère into the crust of a fruit pie. At the time I thought it sounded strange, but it stuck with me, so much so that when I started cooking for myself I tried it. The nutty, mild taste of Gruyère is the perfect complement for the clean crisp taste of apples, and takes these hand pies from simply delicious to stunningly good.

FOR THE FILLING

2 cups peeled Granny Smith apples,
    thinly sliced then cut in half

2 tablespoons packed brown sugar

1 tablespoon granulated sugar

1 tablespoon unsalted butter

¼ teaspoon ground cinnamon

⅛ teaspoon ground nutmeg

Pinch salt

FOR THE CRUST

1 recipe All-Butter Buttermilk Pie
    Crust for a double crust (page 161),
    modified according to step 1

¼ cup grated Gruyère cheese

All-purpose flour, for flouring the
    work surface and the rolling pin

FOR THE EGG WASH

1 large egg

1 tablespoon milk

TO MAKE THE FILLING

In a 2-quart saucepan over medium heat, combine the apples, brown sugar, granulated sugar, butter, cinnamon, nutmeg, and salt. Bring to a simmer and cook for 6 minutes until the apples are soft. Set aside to cool for at least 15 minutes until no longer hot to the touch.

TO MAKE THE CRUST

1. Prepare the pie crust as directed on page 161, but mix in the Gruyère cheese after cutting in the butter, and before stirring in the buttermilk. You may need to add up to 2 teaspoons of buttermilk when preparing. Wrap and chill according to the instructions.

2. Preheat the oven to 425°F.

3. Line a baking sheet with parchment paper.

4. On a well-floured surface and with a floured rolling pin, roll out the dough to a ¼-inch thickness. With a 4-inch biscuit cutter or glass, cut out 10 rounds, gathering the scraps and rerolling the dough as necessary.

5. If the apples are not yet cool, place the rounds on the prepared baking sheet and refrigerate until they are.

TO MAKE THE EGG WASH

Whisk the egg and milk. Brush the egg wash over each round.

TO MAKE THE HAND PIES

1. Top half of the rounds with mounds of apple, leaving a ½-inch border.

2. Top with the remaining rounds, egg wash–side down, and crimp the edges tightly with a fork.

3. Brush the tops with egg wash and use a knife to cut 3 slits in the top of each.

4. Bake for 12 to 16 minutes until golden.

5. Cool for 5 minutes before eating.

Ingredient Tip Gruyère is a bit pricy to buy just for hand pies. If you aren't sure you'll use it for other things, substitute sharp Cheddar cheese. The taste is different, but its tangy, salty flavor goes very well with the apples.

baking sheet

PREP TIME
30 minutes

COOK TIME
28 to 36 minutes

COOLING OR
CHILLING TIME
5 minutes

SHELF LIFE
3 to 4 days

Beef Hand Pies (Pasties)

MAKES 2 hand pies

There is something wonderful about buttery pie crust wrapped around a savory filling. The filling here is a tasty mixture of beef, onions, carrots, potatoes, and rosemary. It's simple to make, and simply mouth-watering when stuffed inside a buttermilk pie crust. The best part about these? The filling is fully cooked before you bake it inside the dough so you don't have to worry about undercooked meat or vegetables. And you can eat any left-overs while you wait for the main event to come out of the oven.

FOR THE FILLING

2 tablespoons unsalted
 butter, divided

1 cup diced (½ inch) beef chuck for
 stewing (about 6 ounces)

¾ cup diced (½ inch) potatoes

¼ cup diced (¼ inch) carrots

1 to 2 cups water

¼ teaspoon salt, plus more as needed

¼ teaspoon crushed dried rosemary

⅛ teaspoon freshly ground black
 pepper, plus more as needed

⅛ teaspoon dried oregano

¼ cup diced onion

1 tablespoon all-purpose flour,
 plus more for flouring the work
 surface and the rolling pin

FOR THE EGG WASH

1 large egg

1 tablespoon milk

FOR THE CRUST

1 recipe All-Butter Buttermilk Pie
 Crust for a double crust (page 161)

1. Preheat the oven to 400°F.

2. Line a baking sheet with parchment paper.

TO MAKE THE FILLING

1. In a 2-quart saucepan over medium heat, melt 1 tablespoon of butter. Add the beef and cook for 4 to 6 minutes until well browned.

2. Add the potatoes and carrots and just enough water to cover them completely. Sprinkle in the salt, rosemary, pepper, and oregano. Bring to a boil and reduce the heat to low. Simmer for 5 minutes just until the potatoes are barely fork-tender and the meat is cooked through. Strain the broth into a separate container and set aside. Set the meat and vegetables aside.

3. In another 2-quart saucepan, melt the remaining 1 tablespoon of butter. Add the onion and cook for 2 to 4 minutes until the edges begin to turn translucent.

4. Stir in the flour and cook for about 1 minute, whisking constantly until a thick paste forms and turns lightly golden. Whisk in ½ cup of the reserved broth, continuing to stir until a thick gravy forms. Taste and add more salt and pepper, if necessary.

5. Stir in the cooked meat and vegetables until everything is well coated. Set the mixture aside to cool.

TO MAKE THE EGG WASH

In a small bowl, whisk the egg and milk. Set aside.

CONTINUED

TO MAKE THE CRUST

1. On a well-floured surface and with a floured rolling pin, roll out 1 ball of dough to just over a ¼-inch thickness. If the dough is a fairly tidy circle, leave it as is; if it is ragged, use a 6-inch bowl as a giant cookie cutter and cut around it for a perfect circle. Transfer the dough to the prepared sheet.

2. Brush some egg wash around the outside inch of the dough. Spoon half the beef mixture over slightly less than half of the dough, leaving a ½-inch space around the edges. Fold the uncovered half of the dough over the filling. With a fork, crimp the dough shut. Cut 4 slits in the top to allow steam to escape and brush with egg wash. Repeat with the second dough ball and the remaining beef mixture.

3. Bake for 15 to 20 minutes until golden.

4. Cool on the sheet for at least 5 minutes before serving.

Cooking Tip These pasties freeze well for an easy lunch or dinner. Freeze the baked pasty on a plate until solid and then wrap tightly in plastic wrap, place in a freezer bag, and store in the freezer for up to 3 months. When you are ready to eat, the frozen pasty can go directly into the microwave for 1 to 3 minutes on high, and should come out with almost no loss of quality in texture or taste.

Sweet Tart Shells

MAKES 2 (4¾-inch) round tarts

This quick and easy tart base gives you the perfect crust for any sweet tart. It comes together with little fuss and bakes up hard and sturdy with a slight cookie crunch to it. Just barely sweetened, it's a mild, buttery, blank canvas just waiting for you to fill it.

½ cup all-purpose flour, plus more for flouring the work surface and the rolling pin

1 tablespoon plus 1 teaspoon granulated sugar

⅛ teaspoon salt

3 tablespoons cold unsalted butter, diced

1½ teaspoons egg yolk

1½ teaspoons ice water

¼ teaspoon vanilla extract

1. In a small bowl, stir together the flour, sugar, and salt.

2. With a pastry blender, two knives, or your fingers, cut the butter into the flour until no pieces larger than a pea remain.

3. Add the egg yolk, ice water, and vanilla. With a fork, stir the mixture until the liquid is completely incorporated and a sticky dough clumps and forms. Squeeze the dough into a ball, wrap it tightly in plastic wrap, and press it into a disk. Refrigerate for 30 minutes.

4. Preheat the oven to 400°F.

CONTINUED

2 (4¾-inch) round tart pans

PREP TIME
10 minutes

COOK TIME
13 to 15 minutes

COOLING OR CHILLING TIME
30 minutes

SHELF LIFE
3 to 4 days

5. Split the dough into 2 balls and return one to the refrigerator while you work. On a well-floured surface and with a floured rolling pin, roll out the dough (adding more flour as needed) so it is about 1 inch wider than the tart pan. Drape the dough over the pan and press it down so it fits snugly at the bottom and sides. Press the dough into the grooves on the side all the way around. Very lightly roll the rolling pin over the top of the pan to cut off the excess dough. If you have any tears or holes, use a thin scrap of dough and a little water as a patch. Repeat with the remaining dough and pan.

6. Place the tart shells on a baking sheet. Place a sheet of parchment paper, cut slightly larger than the tart pan, over each crust and weigh it down with pie weights, dried beans, or rice.

7. Blind bake the crusts for 10 minutes before removing the weights and parchment. Bake for 3 to 5 minutes more until set and the edges are lightly browned.

8. Cool completely before removing from the tart pans and filling.

Cooking Tip Tart shells can be baked up to 48 hours in advance. Keep refrigerated in an airtight container until you are ready to use them.

Strawberry and Cream Cheese Tart

MAKES 2 (4¾-inch) tarts

This elegant tart looks good and tastes fantastic. You start with a buttery tart shell, fill it with a silky mixture of cream, cream cheese, and sugar, spiral some sliced strawberries over the top, and finish by brushing warm jam over the berries for a little glisten.

2 ounces cream cheese,
   at room temperature

1 tablespoon granulated sugar

¼ teaspoon vanilla extract

¼ cup heavy (whipping) cream

2 Sweet Tart Shells (page 189)

½ cup thinly sliced fresh strawberries

1 tablespoon strawberry jam

1. In a small bowl, whisk the cream cheese, sugar, and vanilla until smooth.

2. Whisk in the cream until silky. Evenly divide the filling between the tart shells.

3. Arrange the strawberry slices in a spiral, starting from the outside working in so they slowly build to a small mound in the center.

4. In a small microwave-safe bowl, microwave the jam for 15 to 20 seconds on high until warm and syrupy. Lightly brush the warm jam over the strawberries.

5. Chill for at least 30 minutes before eating.

Variation Tip Any fruit or jam whose flavor pairs well with cream cheese will work in these tarts.

2 (4¾-inch)
round tart pans

PREP TIME
10 minutes

COOK TIME
0 minutes

COOLING OR
CHILLING TIME
30 minutes

SHELF LIFE
2 to 3 days

Lemon Tart with Whipped Cream

2 (4¾-inch)
round tart pans

PREP TIME
10 minutes

COOK TIME
6 to 10 minutes

COOLING OR
CHILLING TIME
1 hour

SHELF LIFE
2 to 3 days

MAKES 2 (4¾-inch) tarts

Bright, tart lemon curd mellowed with barely sweet whipped cream and a crunchy tart base is beyond delicious. Lemon curd might seem a little intimidating at first, but, once you give it a try you'll see it's about as simple as you can get. Lemon juice, eggs, and sugar are whisked together over lightly simmering water until they become a thick, fabulous filling. Stir in a little lemon zest for added punch and butter for richness and you have one tasty tart on your hands.

2 large eggs

¼ cup granulated sugar

¼ cup freshly squeezed lemon juice

2 tablespoons unsalted butter,
    at room temperature

½ teaspoon packed grated lemon zest

2 Sweet Tart Shells (page 189)

½ cup Whipped Cream
    (page 130, half recipe)

1. In the top of a double boiler over lightly simmering water, whisk the eggs, sugar, and lemon juice until combined. Continue whisking for 6 to 10 minutes until the mixture becomes thick and custardy. Pour through a fine-mesh strainer and immediately stir in the butter and lemon zest. Evenly divide the filling between the tart shells and refrigerate for at least 1 hour.

2. Top with whipped cream and serve.

Cooking Tip If you don't own a double boiler, make your own with a heat-proof bowl and saucepan. Simmer 1 inch of water in the saucepan and set the bowl over the top, making sure that the bowl's bottom does not touch the water. Make the recipe as directed.

Caprese Tart

MAKES 2 (4¾-inch) tarts

For savory tarts, my buttermilk pie crust makes a phenomenal base. You get all that flaky, crunchy texture in cute little tart form. And these tarts are a cinch to make. A spoonful of pesto, slices of mozzarella, a handful of sliced cherry tomatoes and you have yourself a quick and easy appetizer or light lunch.

1 recipe All-Butter Buttermilk Pie
    Crust for 2 tart shells (page 161),
    blind baked (see page 162)
2 tablespoons prepared pesto

1½ ounces mozzarella cheese, sliced
2 to 4 cherry tomatoes, sliced
2 fresh basil leaves, thinly sliced

1. Preheat the oven to 400°F.

2. Place the prepared tart shells, still in their tart pans, on a baking sheet. Spread each tart with 1 tablespoon of pesto.

3. Evenly divide the mozzarella cheese between the tarts and top with the tomato slices and basil leaves.

4. Bake for 14 to 17 minutes until the crust is golden and the cheese is bubbly.

5. Cool for 5 minutes before serving.

Ingredient Tip Pesto is another ingredient that freezes well for later use. Freeze leftovers in tablespoon-size portions in an ice cube tray lined with plastic wrap. Once frozen solid, store the pesto cubes in a freezer bag for up to 3 months. The cubes will thaw in 15 to 20 minutes at room temperature.

2 (4¾-inch)
round tart pans,
baking sheet

PREP TIME
5 minutes

COOK TIME
14 to 17 minutes

COOLING OR
CHILLING TIME
5 minutes

SHELF LIFE
2 to 3 days

Sunny-Side Up Tarts

2 (4¾-inch)
round tart pans,
baking sheet

PREP TIME
15 minutes

COOK TIME
14 to 22 minutes

COOLING OR
CHILLING TIME
5 minutes

SHELF LIFE
2 to 3 days

MAKES 2 (4¾-inch) tarts

Tarts for breakfast? Why not? These cuties will add a little sunshine to any morning. Start with a buttermilk pie crust base sprinkled with Cheddar cheese and topped with roasted red bell peppers. Then crack an egg over the top, give it a pinch of salt, a pinch of pepper, maybe a couple shakes of cayenne pepper, and bake just until the cheese is melted and the egg is cooked. Add a little green with some scallions and this is a perfect way to start a perfect morning.

Butter or shortening, for
    greasing the baking sheet
¼ red bell pepper, seeds removed
1 recipe All-Butter Buttermilk Pie
    Crust for 2 tart shells (page 161),
    blind baked (see page 162)

4 tablespoons shredded
    Cheddar cheese
2 large eggs
Pinch salt
Pinch freshly ground black pepper
Pinch cayenne pepper (optional)
1 teaspoon diced scallions

1. Turn the broiler to high.

2. Lightly grease an aluminum foil–covered baking sheet.

3. Trim the rounded top and bottom from the bell pepper. Press the pepper down with the palm of your hand so it lies flat, and transfer it, skin-side up, to the prepared sheet.

4. Broil for 4 to 8 minutes until the skin is bubbly and the flesh underneath is slightly softened. Cut into strips and set aside.

5. Reduce the oven temperature to 400°F.

6. Place the prepared tart shells, still in their tart pans, on a baking sheet.

7. Evenly divide the Cheddar cheese between the shells. Lay the red pepper slices in a row over the cheese.

8. Crack an egg over the top of each, so the yolk rests over the pepper slices in the center of the tart. Season with salt, black pepper, and cayenne pepper (if using).

9. Bake for 10 to 14 minutes until the whites of the eggs are set.

10. Sprinkle with the scallions and cool for 5 minutes before serving.

Cooking Tip The bell pepper strips give the eggs something to rest on so they sit prettily in the center of the tart. If you don't like bell peppers, omit them, but the egg yolk might slide around a bit.

CHAPTER EIGHT

Gratins, Stratas, Quiches & Soufflés

From rich dinner gratins to cheesy breakfast quiches and sweet and savory soufflés, this chapter has you covered for breakfast, lunch, dinner, and dessert. And if some of the recipes sound a little intimidating, don't worry, they're easier than they seem!

Tips & Techniques

Looking for inexpensive cheese options, a richer quiche, or the secret to the tallest, most beautiful soufflé possible? I have just the tips and techniques for you. Read on.

Cheese Please A couple of the cheeses used in this chapter, such as Emmentaler and pecorino romano, are on the pricy side for a small-batch recipe if you don't usually keep them stocked. These recipes are very flexible, so you can use any cheese you like for any of them. Parmesan makes a suitable substitute for pecorino romano, and while very different in taste, Cheddar can be quite tasty everywhere Emmentaler is used in this chapter.

Richer Quiche The quiche recipes in this chapter are all made with milk in the custard. For a richer final product, substitute half-and-half or heavy (whipping) cream in a one-to-one ratio.

Buttering Soufflé Ramekins Both soufflé recipes are baked in buttered soufflé dishes. You can help your soufflés get the tallest rise with this simple technique: When you butter the sides of the dish, swipe the butter on in smooth upward strokes from the bottom all the way to the top. This gives the soufflé a path to follow as it rises, ensuring a tall and beautiful finished product.

Testing for Doneness

The quiches, like the custards from chapter 7, should look slightly puffed up and set around the edges, but with a little jiggle in the center. You can use a thermometer to test the large quiches. It should register between 165°F and 185°F.

Storing

Store the dishes in this chapter covered in the refrigerator. The quiches freeze and reheat well and can be kept tightly wrapped in the freezer for up to 2 months. To reheat, place frozen leftovers into a cold oven. Set the oven to 350°F and bake until warmed through—begin checking after 15 minutes; it will probably take 20 to 30 minutes to fully heat. Cover with aluminum foil if the crust becomes too brown.

Make Your Own Custom Quiche

Do you have a dream of a quiche recipe in your heart? Quiches are endlessly adaptable and creating your own custom recipe is as simple as it is satisfying. All you need is about a cup of preferred quiche fillings and a good base recipe to get you started. To make your own:

1. Preheat the oven to 350°F. Start with my All-Butter Buttermilk Pie Crust for a single crust (page 161), blind baked (page 162), and add ¾ to 1 cup mixture of cheese, cooked meat, and cooked vegetables of your choice.
2. In a small bowl, whisk together 2 large eggs, ¼ cup milk (half-and-half or heavy cream will work too), ¼ teaspoon salt, ⅛ teaspoon pepper, and any other spices that strike your fancy.
3. Pour the egg mixture into the pie crust over the filling. Stop before the mixture reaches the top of the crust—you may not need all the custard. Then just bake until the edges look set but the center still has a bit of a wobble to it, usually 20 to 25 minutes. Cool for 5 to 10 minutes and enjoy your creation!

5-by-7-inch baking dish

PREP TIME
15 minutes

COOK TIME
40 to 50 minutes

COOLING OR
CHILLING TIME
5 minutes

SHELF LIFE
2 to 3 days

Scalloped Potatoes au Gratin

MAKES 1 (5-by-7-inch) gratin

There is no comfort food more perfect than potatoes au gratin. Cheese, ham, potatoes, butter, and just a bit of cream go into the oven and something magical comes out. You're going to love how easy this is to make, and you're going to hate waiting for it to cook. But it's worth the wait, because when it's done, the cheese is browned and bubbly, the ham has little crispy edges to it, and the cream and butter have seeped into the potatoes making them so rich and tender they practically melt in your mouth.

12 ounces potatoes, peeled and thinly sliced, divided

1 cup grated sharp Cheddar cheese, divided

½ cup diced cooked ham, divided

2 tablespoons unsalted butter, diced, divided

1 tablespoon all-purpose flour

¼ teaspoon salt

¼ teaspoon freshly ground black pepper

¼ cup half-and-half

1. Preheat the oven to 400°F.

2. Place half of the potatoes in the baking dish, covering the bottom.

3. Sprinkle ½ cup of Cheddar cheese and ¼ cup of ham over the potatoes.

4. Scatter 1 tablespoon of butter over the top, followed by the flour, salt, and pepper.

5. Layer the remaining potatoes, cheese, ham, and butter over the top and pour in the half-and-half.

6. Bake for 40 to 50 minutes until the cheese is browned and bubbly and the potatoes are tender.

7. Cool for at least 5 minutes before serving.

Ingredient Tip If you don't have half-and-half, substitute 3 tablespoons milk and 1 tablespoon heavy (whipping) cream, or simply use milk.

Macaroni and Cheese Gratin

MAKES 1 (5-by-7-inch) gratin

Macaroni and cheese is the king of carbolicious dishes and surprisingly easy to make, for something most of us grew up making out of a box. Adding a crunchy baked bread crumb and cheese topping is but the work of a moment—but such a delicious upgrade. You didn't think mac and cheese could get any better, but it just did.

5-by-7-inch
baking dish

PREP TIME
15 minutes

COOK TIME
23 to 30 minutes

COOLING OR
CHILLING TIME
5 minutes

SHELF LIFE
2 to 3 days

5 ounces macaroni

2 tablespoons unsalted butter

2 tablespoons all-purpose flour

1 cup milk

1 cup grated sharp Cheddar
cheese, divided

¼ cup grated pecorino romano
cheese, divided

⅛ teaspoon salt, plus more as needed

⅛ teaspoon freshly ground black
pepper, plus more as needed

⅛ teaspoon cayenne pepper

Pinch nutmeg

Pinch paprika

¼ cup bread crumbs

1. Preheat the oven to 400°F.

2. Cook the macaroni al dente, according to the package instructions. Drain, transfer to a medium bowl, and set aside.

3. In a 2-quart saucepan over medium heat, melt the butter. Whisk in the flour and cook for about 1 minute until lightly browned.

4. Slowly whisk in the milk, beating out any lumps that form. Continue to cook for 3 to 6 minutes over medium heat until the mixture is thick and bubbly. Remove from the heat, stir in ¾ cup of Cheddar cheese and 3 tablespoons of pecorino romano cheese. Season with salt, black pepper, cayenne pepper, nutmeg, and paprika. Taste and adjust the seasonings, if necessary.

CONTINUED

5. Pour the cheese sauce over the macaroni and stir to coat, then transfer to the baking dish.

6. Sprinkle with the remaining ¼ cup of Cheddar cheese.

7. In a small bowl, stir together the remaining tablespoon of pecorino romano cheese and the bread crumbs. Sprinkle this over the top of the macaroni.

8. Bake for 8 to 12 minutes until the cheese is melted and the crumbs look toasted.

9. Cool for 5 minutes before serving.

Ingredient Tip If you don't have bread crumbs handy, make your own by lightly toasting a slice of bread and grating it on a cheese grater. One slice of bread will make more than enough for the ¼ cup this recipe requires.

Asparagus Gratin

MAKES 2 servings

For those times when you need an easy cheesy side, give this one a try. Fresh asparagus is coated with a bit of butter, a healthy sprinkle of cheese, and bread crumbs for a crunchy, cheesy vegetable experience. No one will refuse to eat veggies that taste this good.

Cooking spray

12 asparagus spears, washed and
    tough ends trimmed

1 tablespoon unsalted butter, melted

Salt

Freshly ground black pepper

½ cup shredded mozzarella cheese

2 tablespoons Parmesan cheese,
    or pecorino romano cheese

2 tablespoons bread crumbs

baking sheet

PREP TIME
5 minutes

COOK TIME
8 to 12 minutes

COOLING OR
CHILLING TIME
0 minutes

SHELF LIFE
serve immediately

1. Preheat the oven to 400°F.

2. Line a baking sheet with aluminum foil and spray it with cooking spray.

3. Arrange the asparagus on the prepared sheet so the spears are lying side by side, touching. Drizzle with the melted butter and season with salt and pepper.

4. Sprinkle the mozzarella in the middle of the spears, leaving the heads mostly bare.

5. In a small bowl, stir together the Parmesan and bread crumbs. Sprinkle this over the mozzarella.

6. Bake for 8 to 12 minutes until the cheese is melted and the asparagus is tender.

Variation Tip You can lighten this dish by omitting the butter and mozzarella. Drizzle about 1 teaspoon extra-virgin olive oil over the spears instead of butter, and sprinkle with salt, pepper, Parmesan cheese, and bread crumbs for a less cheesy, but still delicious, dish.

Ham and Cheese Croissant Strata

MAKES 1 (5-by-7-inch) strata

5-by-7-inch
baking dish

PREP TIME
10 minutes

COOK TIME
20 to 30 minutes

COOLING OR
CHILLING TIME
4 hours, 35 minutes

SHELF LIFE
1 to 2 days

The great thing about stratas is they are at their best when made the night before so the chunks of bread tossed with eggs and cream have time to soak up all that amazing liquid. This means they are the perfect lazy morning breakfast. Assemble it before you turn in and pop it in the oven the next morning and you have a delicious hot breakfast without lifting a knife. This version uses croissants, cubed, and tossed with ham, cheese, and scallions. Breakfast in bed never tasted so good.

Butter or shortening, for
    greasing the baking dish

3 cups cubed croissants

½ cup shredded Cheddar
    cheese, divided

½ cup diced cooked ham

1 small scallion, thinly sliced

2 large eggs

½ cup milk

¼ teaspoon salt

⅛ teaspoon freshly ground
    black pepper

1. Grease the baking dish.

2. In a large bowl, combine the croissant pieces, ¼ cup of Cheddar cheese, the ham, and scallion. Toss lightly to mix.

3. In a small bowl, whisk the eggs, milk, salt, and pepper. Pour this mixture over the croissant pieces and toss to coat. Transfer to the prepared dish and sprinkle with the remaining ¼ cup of Cheddar cheese. Cover the dish and refrigerate for at least 4 hours, or up to 12 hours.

4. Remove the strata from the refrigerator at least 30 minutes before baking.

5. Preheat the oven to 350°F.

6. Bake the strata for 20 to 30 minutes until the top is crispy and a knife inserted into the center comes out clean. The finished dish should be moist, but not runny.

7. Cool for 5 minutes before serving.

Variation Tip Substitute any fully cooked meat you like for the ham and use white bread instead of croissants.

Cinnamon French Toast Strata

MAKES 1 (5-by-7-inch) strata

This is one of my childhood favorites reimagined as a breakfast strata. White bread is tossed with butter and cinnamon sugar before being coated in custard and sprinkled with a little (a lot) more cinnamon sugar. The top comes out toasted and cinnamon sweet and the bottom is rich and custardy with swirls of cinnamon throughout. It's as pretty to look at as it is tasty to eat.

FOR THE CINNAMON TOPPING

1 tablespoon granulated sugar

¼ teaspoon ground cinnamon

FOR THE FRENCH TOAST

1 tablespoon unsalted butter, melted, plus more for greasing the baking dish

3 tablespoons granulated sugar, divided

1 teaspoon ground cinnamon

4 cups cubed good-quality white bread (about 4 slices)

2 large eggs

½ cup milk

½ teaspoon vanilla extract

Pinch salt

5-by-7-inch baking dish

PREP TIME
10 minutes

COOK TIME
20 to 30 minutes

COOLING OR CHILLING TIME
4 hours, 35 minutes

SHELF LIFE
1 to 2 days

TO MAKE THE CINNAMON TOPPING

In a small bowl, stir together the sugar and cinnamon. Set aside.

TO MAKE THE FRENCH TOAST

1. Grease the baking dish.

2. In a large bowl, stir together the butter, 1 tablespoon of sugar, and the cinnamon.

3. Add the bread cubes and toss to coat, making sure to mix well.

CONTINUED

4. In a small bowl, whisk the eggs, milk, the remaining 2 tablespoons of sugar, the vanilla, and salt. Pour this mixture over the bread and stir to combine. Transfer the mixture to the prepared dish.

5. Sprinkle the topping over the strata. Cover and refrigerate for at least 4 hours, or up to 12.

6. Remove the strata from the refrigerator at least 30 minutes before baking.

7. Preheat the oven to 375°F.

8. Bake for 20 to 30 minutes until the top is toasty and a knife inserted into the center comes out clean.

9. Cool for 5 minutes before serving.

Variation Tip This dish is meant to be served without additional toppings. If you would like to serve it with syrup, omit or greatly reduce the cinnamon sugar topping.

Strawberry and Cream Cheese Strata

MAKES 1 (5-by-7-inch) strata

Fresh strawberries and tangy, lightly sweetened cream cheese sandwiched between layers of custard-soaked bread make an almost unbelievably out-of-this-world breakfast. Serve with a light drizzle of real maple syrup, and reserve this one for special occasions.

5-by-7-inch
baking dish

PREP TIME
10 minutes

COOK TIME
20 to 30 minutes

COOLING OR
CHILLING TIME
4 hours, 35 minutes

SHELF LIFE
1 to 2 days

Butter or shortening, for
   greasing the baking dish

2 ounces cream cheese,
   at room temperature

3 tablespoons granulated sugar,
   plus 2 teaspoons, divided

2 large eggs

½ cup milk

½ teaspoon vanilla extract

⅛ teaspoon salt

4 cups cubed good-quality
   white bread (about 4 slices)

½ cup chopped fresh
   strawberries, divided

Powdered sugar, for
   topping (optional)

Maple syrup, for topping (optional)

1. Grease the baking dish.

2. In a small bowl, whisk the cream cheese and 2 teaspoons of granulated sugar. Set aside.

3. In a large bowl, whisk the eggs, milk, the remaining 3 tablespoons of granulated sugar, the vanilla, and salt.

4. Add the bread cubes to the large bowl and toss to coat. Transfer half of the bread mixture to the prepared dish.

5. Drop dollops of the sweetened cream cheese over the bread.

CONTINUED

6. Sprinkle ¼ cup of strawberries over the top, followed by the remaining bread mixture.

7. Sprinkle with the remaining ¼ cup of strawberries. Cover and refrigerate for 4 hours, or up to 12 hours.

8. Remove the strata from the refrigerator at least 30 minutes before baking.

9. Preheat the oven to 350°F.

10. Bake for 20 to 30 minutes until the top is crunchy and a knife inserted into the center comes out clean.

11. Cool for 5 minutes before serving dusted with powdered sugar (if using) or drizzled with maple syrup (if using).

Variation Tip Once you've made this with strawberries, try some of your other favorite fruits—perhaps fresh blueberries or peaches.

Quiche Lorraine

MAKES 1 (6-inch) quiche

Quiche Lorraine is a simple quiche made with Gruyère or Swiss cheese, bacon, and spinach. It looks great on your brunch table, and tastes even better.

6-inch pie pan

PREP TIME
20 minutes

COOK TIME
20 to 25 minutes

COOLING OR
CHILLING TIME
5 minutes

SHELF LIFE
2 to 3 days

4 bacon slices

1 cup roughly chopped fresh spinach

1 large scallion, chopped

½ cup grated Emmentaler cheese, divided

1 recipe All-Butter Buttermilk Pie Crust for a single crust (page 161), blind baked (see page 162)

2 large eggs

¼ cup milk

¼ teaspoon salt

⅛ teaspoon freshly ground black pepper

⅛ teaspoon ground nutmeg

Pinch paprika

1. Preheat the oven to 350°F.

2. In a large pan, cook the bacon over medium heat until crisp. Transfer the bacon to a paper towel–lined plate and set aside. Pour off the bacon grease from the pan and add the chopped spinach. Cook over medium heat until wilted, 1 to 2 minutes. Remove the pan from the heat. Crumble or roughly chop the bacon.

3. Sprinkle the bacon, spinach, scallion, and ¼ cup of Emmentaler cheese over the bottom of the pie crust.

4. In a small bowl, whisk the eggs, milk, salt, pepper, nutmeg, and paprika. Pour this mixture into the pie crust over the cheese mixture. Sprinkle the remaining ¼ cup of cheese on top.

5. Bake for 20 to 25 minutes until the top barely jiggles and the crust is golden.

6. Cool for at least 5 minutes before cutting and serving.

Variation Tip I like to use scallions for their green color and because they don't require cooking first. If you like, substitute white or yellow onions. Use ¼ cup chopped onion and cook it until slightly softened before adding it to the quiche.

Broccoli and Cheddar Quiche

MAKES 1 (6-inch) quiche

6-inch pie pan

PREP TIME
20 minutes

COOK TIME
28 to 35 minutes

COOLING OR
CHILLING TIME
5 minutes

SHELF LIFE
2 to 3 days

Yes, broccoli can be a breakfast food if you try hard enough . . . or not very hard at all. It makes a surprisingly great quiche addition when baked with ham, Cheddar cheese, and onions. Serve it for breakfast for a nice early morning veggie boost or add it to your meal rotation as an easy dinner for two.

1 tablespoon unsalted butter

¼ cup diced onion

1 garlic clove, minced

½ cup diced cooked ham

1½ cups medium-dice broccoli

1 tablespoon water

1 recipe All-Butter Buttermilk Pie
    Crust for a single crust (page 161),
    blind baked (page 162)

2 large eggs

¼ cup milk

¼ teaspoon salt

⅛ teaspoon freshly ground
    black pepper

¼ teaspoon paprika

⅛ teaspoon ground nutmeg

½ cup grated sharp Cheddar
    cheese, divided

1. Preheat the oven to 350°F.

2. In a medium skillet over medium heat, melt the butter.

3. Add the onion and cook for 2 to 4 minutes until translucent.

4. Stir in the garlic and cook for 30 seconds until lightly toasted. Add the ham, broccoli, and water. Cook for 4 to 5 minutes, stirring frequently, until the water evaporates and the broccoli is tender. Pour this mixture into the prepared pie crust.

5. In a medium bowl, whisk the eggs, milk, salt, pepper, paprika, and nutmeg. Stir in ¼ cup of Cheddar. Pour this mixture over the broccoli (some of the broccoli will not be submerged) and top with the remaining ¼ cup of Cheddar.

6. Bake for 20 to 25 minutes until the top is golden and barely jiggly.

7. Cool for at least 5 minutes before cutting and serving.

Variation Tip This is a great way to use up leftover steamed broccoli from dinner. If using precooked broccoli, omit the water and toss the broccoli in the pan just long enough for it to heat up, then mix with the other ingredients. Any mild cooked vegetable, such as zucchini or asparagus, also does well here.

Bite-Size Mini Vegetarian Quiches

mini muffin tin

PREP TIME
20 minutes

COOK TIME
24 to 29 minutes

COOLING OR
CHILLING TIME
5 minutes

SHELF LIFE
2 to 3 days

MAKES 10 mini quiches

These little quiches are packed to the brim, literally, with fresh veggies and salty feta cheese. Topped with a single cherry tomato slice, they make an easy addition to any brunch, although they are almost too cute to eat.

Cooking spray, for greasing the tins if they are not nonstick

All-purpose flour, for flouring the work surface and the rolling pin

1 recipe All-Butter Buttermilk Pie Crust for a single crust (page 161)

¼ cup finely diced onion

½ cup finely chopped fresh spinach

2 tablespoons crumbled feta cheese

1 large egg

2 tablespoons milk

⅛ teaspoon salt

⅛ teaspoon freshly ground black pepper

10 cherry tomato slices

1. Preheat the oven to 400°F.

2. Spray a mini muffin tin with cooking spray.

3. On a well-floured surface and with a floured rolling pin, roll out the dough to a ⅛-inch thickness and cut out 10 (2½-inch) rounds. Press the rounds into the mini muffin tin. Bake for 10 minutes until the crusts are lightly golden. Remove from the oven and use the back of a wooden spoon to poke down the centers where they have puffed up.

4. Spray a small skillet with cooking spray and place it over medium heat.

5. Add the onion and cook for 2 to 3 minutes until softened.

6. Add the spinach and cook for 1 to 2 minutes until wilted and dark green. Spoon about 1 teaspoon of spinach and onion into each crust, followed by a sprinkle of feta cheese.

7. In a large liquid measuring cup or other container with a lip for pouring, whisk the egg, milk, salt, and pepper. Pour this custard over the feta, filling the crust just to the top. Do not overfill! Press a slice of tomato into each.

8. Bake for 11 to 14 minutes until the crusts are golden.

9. Cool for 5 minutes before serving.

Ingredient Tip No cherry tomatoes? No problem. Finely dice whatever tomato you have on hand and sprinkle it over the top, or omit the tomato completely.

Bite-Size Smoked Salmon Quiches

mini muffin tin

PREP TIME
20 minutes

COOK TIME
21 to 24 minutes

COOLING OR
CHILLING TIME
5 minutes

SHELF LIFE
2 to 3 days

MAKES 10 mini quiches

These salmon quiches are dangerous because you can't just pop one into your mouth and stop. Nutty Emmentaler cheese brings out the best in smoked salmon, and together they make a delicious and delectable bite-size appetizer.

Butter or shortening, for greasing
    the muffin tin

All-purpose flour, for flouring the
    work surface and the rolling pin

1 recipe All-Butter Buttermilk Pie
    Crust for a single crust (page 161)

2 ounces smoked salmon,
    torn into pieces

1 large egg

2 tablespoons milk

⅛ teaspoon salt

⅛ teaspoon freshly ground
    black pepper

Pinch dried dill

¼ cup grated Emmentaler cheese

1. Preheat the oven to 400°F.

2. Lightly grease a mini muffin tin.

3. On a well-floured surface and with a floured rolling pin, roll out the dough to a ⅛-inch thickness and cut out 10 (2½-inch) rounds. Press the rounds into the mini muffin tin. Bake for 10 minutes until the crusts are lightly golden. Remove from the oven and use the back of a wooden spoon to poke down the centers where they have puffed up.

4. Place a piece of salmon in the center of each crust.

5. In a large liquid measuring cup or other container with a lip for pouring, whisk the egg, milk, salt, pepper, and dill. Pour over the salmon, filling just to the top of the crust. Do not overfill!

6. Sprinkle the Emmentaler cheese on top of each quiche.

7. Bake for 11 to 14 minutes until the centers are puffed and the crusts are golden.

8. Cool the quiches in the tin for 5 minutes before serving.

Cooking Tip Take care not to overfill your mini quiches. An overflow of the custard can make removing them from the pan after baking a challenge. If you have any trouble removing the mini quiches, use a plastic knife or fork to pop them out so you don't damage the finish on your tin.

2 (12-ounce) ramekins)

PREP TIME
15 minutes

COOK TIME
24 to 31 minutes

COOLING OR
CHILLING TIME
0 minutes

SHELF LIFE
serve immediately

Cheese Soufflé

MAKES 2 (12-ounce) soufflés

Have you ever wanted to eat a cloud of cheese? Because that's more or less what eating one of these cheese soufflés is like. They are light and airy and full of cheesy flavor. Soufflés get a bad rap for being finicky and difficult to make, but if you can whip egg whites, you can absolutely make a soufflé. Give it a go in a low-stress situation just to prove to yourself that you can, then make one for someone you love.

2½ tablespoons unsalted butter, at room temperature, divided

3 tablespoons all-purpose flour

1 cup milk

½ cup grated Cheddar cheese

⅛ teaspoon salt, plus more as needed

⅛ teaspoon freshly ground black pepper, plus more as needed

2 large eggs, at room temperature, separated

Pinch cream of tartar

1 tablespoon grated Parmesan cheese

Fresh oregano, for garnish (optional)

1. Remove the top rack from the oven and preheat the oven to 400°F.

2. With a pastry brush, use ½ tablespoon of butter to coat the inside of the ramekins, covering the bottom and brushing up the sides in long, upward strokes. Refrigerate the ramekins until ready to use.

3. In a 3-quart saucepan over medium heat, melt the remaining 2 tablespoons of butter.

4. Whisk in the flour until lightly brown, about 1 minute.

5. Slowly pour in the milk, whisking continuously for 4 to 6 minutes to avoid lumps and until it thickens and becomes bubbly around the edges. Remove from the heat and stir in the Cheddar cheese, salt, and pepper. Taste and adjust the seasonings, if necessary. Set aside to cool.

6. In a medium bowl, combine the egg whites and cream of tartar. With an electric mixer, beat the whites until stiff peaks form. Refrigerate until needed.

7. Test the cheese mixture. If it is still hot to the touch, let it cool for a few minutes. If just warm, add the egg yolks and whisk until well combined.

8. Remove the whites from the refrigerator. Fold one-third of the whites into the cheese mixture. Fold in the remaining whites in 2 equal batches, stopping when the whites are just combined. Transfer the mixture to the prepared ramekins, filling each three-fourths full. Place them on a baking sheet.

9. Bake on the bottom oven rack for 20 to 25 minutes, or until the tops are tall and a lovely golden brown.

10. Garnish with a sprinkle of Parmesan and oregano (if using), and serve immediately. They will begin to fall shortly after coming out of the oven.

Variation Tip These soufflés are very flexible. Use whatever type of cheese you prefer and add any spices that sound good to you!

Chocolate Soufflé

MAKES 2 (8-ounce) soufflés

2 (8-ounce)
ramekins

PREP TIME
15 minutes

COOK TIME
10 to 13 minutes

COOLING OR
CHILLING TIME
0 minutes

SHELF LIFE
serve immediately

Like savory cheese soufflés, chocolate soufflés are much simpler than their reputation would have you believe. They are well worth the small effort it takes and their rich chocolate texture and almost molten core are something everyone should experience at least once. Just follow the instructions as written and you'll get a perfect soufflé the first time—and every time after that.

2 tablespoons unsalted butter, at
 room temperature, divided

1 tablespoon granulated
 sugar, divided

1 cup (6 ounces) semisweet chocolate

3 large eggs, at room
 temperature, separated

⅛ teaspoon cream of tartar

Powdered sugar, for dusting
 (optional)

1. Remove the top rack from the oven and preheat the oven to 400°F.

2. With a pastry brush, use 1 tablespoon of butter to coat the inside of the ramekins, covering the bottom and brushing up the sides in long, upward strokes. Add 1½ teaspoons of granulated sugar to each and shake so all the butter is coated. Refrigerate the ramekins until ready to use.

3. In a double boiler over barely simmering water, melt the chocolate. Remove from the heat and stir in the remaining 1 tablespoon of butter.

4. In a medium bowl, combine the egg whites and cream of tartar. With an electric mixer, beat the whites until stiff peaks form. Refrigerate until needed.

5. Whisk two egg yolks into the chocolate mixture until smooth. Save the third yolk for another use or discard it.

6. Remove the egg whites from the refrigerator. Fold about one-fourth of the whites into the chocolate mixture. Fold in the remaining whites, in thirds, just until mixed. The mixture will not be a uniform color, but there should be no distinct streaks of white. Divide the mixture, filling each ramekin three-fourths full. Discard any extra batter.

7. Bake on the bottom oven rack for 10 to 13 minutes until lifted nicely.

8. Dust with powdered sugar (if using) and serve immediately as the soufflés will begin to fall just minutes after coming out of the oven.

Cooking Tip As written, these chocolate soufflés have a soft chocolate core. If you prefer a spongy, cake-like texture all the way through, cook for 2 to 3 minutes more.

Measurement Conversion Tables

Volume Equivalents (Liquid)

US STANDARD	US STANDARD (OUNCES)	METRIC (APPROXIMATE)
2 tablespoons	1 fl. oz.	30 mL
¼ cup	2 fl. oz.	60 mL
½ cup	4 fl. oz.	120 mL
1 cup	8 fl. oz.	240 mL
1½ cups	12 fl. oz.	355 mL
2 cups or 1 pint	16 fl. oz.	475 mL
4 cups or 1 quart	32 fl. oz.	1 L
1 gallon	128 fl. oz.	4 L

Oven Temperatures

FAHRENHEIT (F)	CELSIUS (C) (APPROXIMATE)
250°F	120°C
300°F	150°C
325°F	165°C
350°F	180°C
375°F	190°C
400°F	200°C
425°F	220°C
450°F	230°C

Volume Equivalents (Dry)

US STANDARD	METRIC (APPROXIMATE)
¼ teaspoon	1 mL
½ teaspoon	2 mL
1 teaspoon	5 mL
1 tablespoon	15 mL
¼ cup	59 mL
⅓ cup	79 mL
½ cup	118 mL
1 cup	177 mL

Weight Equivalents

US STANDARD	METRIC (APPROXIMATE)
½ ounce	15 g
1 ounce	30 g
2 ounces	60 g
4 ounces	115 g
8 ounces	225 g
12 ounces	340 g
16 ounces or 1 pound	455 g

Equivalent Weights of Common Baking Ingredients

	1 CUP	1 TABLESPOON	1 TEASPOON
All-purpose flour	120g	8g	3g
Cake flour	120g	8g	3g
Sifted cake flour	100g	7g	2g
Sugar (granulated, brown, superfine)	200g	13g	4g
Powdered sugar	120g	8g	3g
Cocoa powder	80g	5g	2g
Chocolate, chopped	168g	11g	4g
Butter	224g	14g	5g

28 grams = 1 ounce

For a more comprehensive list, visit the USDA Food Composition Database
https://ndb.nal.usda.gov/

Recipe Index

Index

Acknowledgments

This book would not exist without my family, who lend me their unwavering support in everything I do in life, even the ridiculous things. You were there with me in the sugar-filled trenches of recipe testing and talked me down from the ledge during the writing process, when I was sure I had exhausted every single way of describing a recipe as delicious. A million times, thank you.

Thank you to friends and family (and occasionally friends of family) for being taste testers and guinea pigs. Your feedback was invaluable.

And thank you to Meg Ilasco and Callisto Media for this opportunity. It has been a delight.

About the Author

Tracy Yabiku is a California-based food writer. She runs the popular food blog *Baking Mischief* where she writes using too many exclamation marks and creates easy and delicious small-batch recipes. You can find her on Twitter and Instagram @BakingMischief.

CPSIA information can be obtained
at www.ICGtesting.com
Printed in the USA
JSHW031156261020
8916JS00005B/5